GOD'S EQUAL LIVING CONDITIONS

JUDGMENT CALL

Gods Equal

Living

Conditions

God's Equal Living Conditions

© Copyright, 2014
by
Prophet Gentle

ISBN – 978-0-9852206-6-2
Library of congress number: 2014939276

All rights reserved. No part of this publication may be reproduced, stored in a retrieval system, or transmitted in any form or by any means, electronic, mechanical, photocopying, recording, or otherwise, without the prior written permission of the author and publisher.

Cover designed by Water for The Journey, Inc.
Photography
Editors

DGPUBLISHING, INC.
2720 Blair Stone Rd.
Tallahassee, FL 32304
www.dgpublishingpress.com
850-566-8169

Acknowledgment

God's supreme existence works through many people in the heavens on earth. Everything that exists in the heavens on earth has its own nature and reason for existence whether good or bad, but without God working spiritually in the inner man of a person, no human would have sense enough to produce anything in the heavens on earth. It is with prime reason God is the first cause for every publishing company in the heavens on earth. God brought nature about before human existence by calling a thing as though it was and it appeared in the heavens on earth and God saw that it was all good. Then God called humankind into being to replenish what the spirits of God started in the heavens on earth.

God's Equal Living Conditions

God then put God's spiritual image in humankind to replenish the earth and have babies. This then brought the world into existence. Supreme reality is the idea of possessing all structural perfection in existence. I Prophet am an ultimate witness to the ultimate relationship between God and humankind spiritual structural reason for existence.

God's Equal Living Conditions

Foreword

by Prophet Gentle

Eternal life now presents the foundational and diverse perspectives on key issues engaged in eternal life in heaven which is on earth. It is more rational to believe God gave us the value for gravity that we have right now in our universe when one reads from the Bible book of Genesis. We got the value that we have when God created heaven on earth. In the beginning God created the heavens on earth. The earth was without form and void, and it was dark on the face of heaven, which is the earth. The spirits of God began to move upon the heavenly earth. It was then God said let the waters under the heavens be gathered together into one place. The dry land then appeared. My justification of eternal life is, I believe in the spiritual realm of eternal of life given me by the spirits of God within me. God is the gravity of strong spiritual forces in the heavens on earth.

The stars and the planet God upholds independently that makes our lives possible. It is my spiritual belief that God's spiritual forces do play a-part in the change of environment that has seasons of complexity of weather in physical, chemical, and biotic forces of factors. These forces mentioned happen along with social and cultural conditions that influence the life of an individual, or community, and the control of the pollution over all the heavens which is the earth. One must give respect entirely with reference to

God's Equal Living Conditions

God in order to explain natural causes of weather, earthquakes, water, and fire which dominate the earth in the call of God's judgment upon the heavens which is on earth.

The existence of the universe cannot be explained without reference to the spiritual forces of God working within the human being spirits and human nature that are in the heavens on earth. God is the spiritual naturalism in the heavens on earth working accomplishments of judgment in the physical and mental of the believer. God's spirits within each person of eternal life is the beginning and the end of all things that exist in the heavens on earth. Genesis book of the Bible explains the natural causes that refer to God the creator and maker of the universe and the people within it. Humankind does not have a way to prove that the spiritual forces of God did not make the heavens on earth. God is spirit saying are ye holy, for I God am holy in spirits and in truth is the spiritual truth.

The systematic world is made by mankind having the spiritual image of God within their heart, mind, body, and soul. God is persistent through the intervention of His divine power independent of humankind in whatever God does in the heavens on earth to get humankind's attention. There are many people who refuse to admit the spiritual power of God cause many things to happen in the earth to exist and to disappear in the heaven on earth. God is the supreme ultimate reality and perfect in spiritual

God's Equal Living Conditions

power, spiritual wisdom, and spiritual goodness. God is worshipped as creator and ruler of the universe overall eternal spirits of the infinite mind of all human being in supreme power as a supreme ruler knowing that his/her power come from the almighty powerful spirits of the inside of the mind, controlling the mind.

God is the independent cause for the independent existence of each personal spirits within every person. The cause of God is spiritual independent cause for the existence of all people, places, and things in the heavens on earth. The people, places, and things that exist depend on God to continue to exist. God can bring a storm and tear down every-thing the spiritual mind thought of to build. The God of independent

God's Equal Living Conditions

cause gave the spiritual mind to each individual to replenish the heavens on earth and do well. Humankind depends on their spiritual mind to comprehend and do things that are within the spiritual mind. It is factual if humankind did not have a spiritual mind; each individual would be lost not knowing how to organize themselves to walk, talk, write, read, drive, labor, and do many other things done in the heavens on earth. There are some people with good spirits, and there are some people with evil spirits. God allows people to make choices, just like Adam and Eve were allowed to make the choice to obey the spirits of God call to their spiritual mind, but they refused to obey what God told them not to do. God allows individuals to choose good or evil. Now

God's Equal Living Conditions

God is bringing all evil to an end into judgment of eternal death beneath the heavens on earth.

All humankind depends on God for all things done in their lives. Now you know without the spiritual being of God within your spirits, you can-not exist. We all that are still living among the land of the living in the heavens on earth are depending on God to bring us through this evil bearing, money stricken, sinful land to eternal life. God is independent spirits and does not need anyone to exist in the heavens on earth, but we need God to exist in the heavens on earth. All people, places, and things in the earth have a real existence in the heavens on earth. All individual spirits are spiritual beings that God's spirits have given us to comprehend existence whether

God's Equal Living Conditions

material or spiritual of humankind we see and hear with our physical being. Everything in the heavens on earth has a reason for being in existence in a specific place even if it has limitations or conditions attached to it. God continues to manifest every mode of being that is now present in the earth.

No-one will ever know the secret ways of God. God covers time and space divinely in the heavens on earth operating the spiritual will of God's power through powerful humankind that God has given power to call a thing as though it were in the heavens on earth and it then comes into existence. These things prophesied are the spiritual being of God daily in the heavens on earth as the righteous people depend on the powerful spirits of their mind that God's spirits introduce to them through spiritual utterance forces and spiritual guidance forces from spiritual forces within them from God. The forces of God and God's people utter peaceful spirits in the heavens daily. It is revealed to the people the insight of God's signs outwardly showed up are the gospel truth of God's laws within judgments and justice. In the earth are now the punishments of God's latter days have arrived upon the people of the chosen generations. These are the days of the promises of God's fulfillment of the holy priests Prophets with words from God that now stand and show up quickly.

The present transactions of God are continued by the direct call of the spirits of God.

God's Equal Living Conditions

The call of God is not in the calculation of humankind of 7000 years of God's judgments and justice called upon the people in every part of the earth from coast to coast. The penetration of Gods words and spirits is in the Holy services of the Holy Temples of God are uncompromising promises guaranteed protection and assurance of God. The latter day transformation stairways to the new paradise earth are daily in the works of God east, west, north, and south in all the earth. The visions of righteousness are being performed through righteous spirits of the people of God seeking eternal life. In place are known conditions that reflects God's promises to cripple the system of unrighteousness with forces of judgments and justice in the earth. Now in its new stages of life

God's Equal Living Conditions

are the things of God's judgments, and justice operation in every part of the earth catches up with the other new stages of life renewing the earth into a paradise earth. In the new changes and different stages of life, God control's human destiny showing genuine change in one's personal life now in the present times of one's life. The change of many cities and counties where people are isolated by groups are identified by economic inheritance are destroyed bringing hardship to many that lost their estates to the call of natural disasters.

The spirits of God and God's people change the world forming daily in every second of the day. The promise of God brings security to equal living on a paradise earth. The bitterness of

God's Equal Living Conditions

the people turns to happiness of trust in God and God's people. The promise of God to send a Prophet to guide the people to eternal life on a paradise earth is here. The Highest Priest Prophet ever to walk the earth in our times and season of now is hear. There will never be another Prophet of the Highest. The promise of the paradise earth with the heavens on earth is taking its form every minute of each day. Things are changing in the blink of an eye right before the face of the people.

It is time for the people to realize that they have been misled and bought with a price that cannot enter eternal life on a peaceful paradise heaven on earth. The people who have focused on the return of Jesus have been misled

God's Equal Living Conditions

by their forefathers' traditions. The people in the days of Jesus added and took messages and spirits of God from the Bible to mislead the people for self-gain as the people of today do. These are reasons why the people in the Bible days and disciples were destroyed never to return to the earth. There will not be any Bibles used when the heavens on earth appear as the peaceful paradise earth without sickness and sin. The Bibles in the earth cease from use as the world form changes to the good of the people. I the Lord your God say to you take my words sent to you serious at heart to enter eternal life on a paradise earth.

God's Equal Living Conditions

Contents

1. The Suffering Conditions Change by the Hands of Time---------7

2. Culture is the Past Conditions---------25

3. The People are Guaranteed Equal Rights--39

4. The End of Stressful Times Surface---------57

5. The Outbreak of God's Power---------75

6. Victory Appears With Heaven on Earth----89

7. All Spirits of the People United---------107

8. The Latter Days Declared Daily---------121

9. The Judgment of God's People Prevail---135

10. The People's Mind Controlled by Spirits Within---------149

11. The Slaughter of Famine Destroyed-----163

12. Spirits of God and God's People Remain Forever---------177

God's Equal Living Conditions

13. Difficult Times Removed from the Heavens Which Is On the Earth------------------------------191

14. Declaring the Truth about God---------205

Introduction

It takes courage to hold visions that are not in the mainstream, but it is exactly that courage to take a stand for one's vision. This book is my visions that distinguish people with high levels of personal mastery in personal spirits of ministry seeing and hearing from God. God is one supreme-being (a person) having super natural powers that has been given to that person by God. God is the internal spiritual being of individuals working external spiritual powers in the earth universally. God is a perfect being in power within the mind of the person and/or people having spirits of supreme ultimate reality

God's Equal Living Conditions

and wisdom spiritually. The spiritual powers and goodness of the person and/or people are worshipped as the creator and ruler of the universe. The spiritual reality over-all are eternal spirits of the infinite mind of a human-being having incorporeal divine principles to rule super natural spirits that attribute to powerful spirits within the infinite mind, but the ownership of the "supernatural spirits is God. There is a person and/or people controlling a particular aspect of reality or part of reality that has been given to him or her from the supernatural spirits of God. This person or people then are of supreme value and a powerful ruler. God is a spiritual supreme being dwelling on the inside of one who believes and lives by faith with works toward living eternal

God's Equal Living Conditions

life. This then gives the person or people free course within because of the supernatural spirits internal and external operating action those things seen and heard in the mind. A person, place, or thing can be of supreme value at any given time. Anyone is free to discuss a subject matter, but belief in God is being free to believe in your own spirits. The spirits of your mind tell you what to do and what not to do; these are spirits of God operating internal inside your mind. The discussion of philosophy does not make one free; anyone is free to believe in their own free-will spirits. There are many people in denial there is a God, which is their own free-will spirits dwelling on the inside of their own mind. The people must understand they guard their own spiritual minds because God allows them to be in control and make good or bad choice as Adam and Eve were given the same "opportunity. Many philosophers aim re-establishing the reality of God and defining the divine nature of laws of God and society while making theory and contradiction in many subject matters. God is the independent cause of everything that exists or has existed. The spirits of God that are your spirits give rise to cause and effect of all people, places, and things in the heavens on earth. These things mentioned are sufficient reasons that give cause to the spiritual minds of the people existing in the heavens on earth are all the spirits of God operating for the good people.

God's Equal Living Conditions

The outward signs of God have showed up in every part of the earth now being revealed to the people. God's judgment calls like never before have formed its justice all over the land. The work of God's spirits is nationally showing the effects of wrath within water, fire, accidents, sinkholes, and death roaming the land in the justice judgments of God's spirits. It is now without fail things happen in an instant are the signs and wonders of God over powering the human judgments bringing the earth to a paradise earth after everyone left living is free from sin. It is now all sins are being dealt with and destroyed in every part of the earth. There be no sin left in the earth when God gets finish calling just judgments and justice in all the earth. The

God's Equal Living Conditions

people know and feel the effects of God's direct actions in all the earth. These are now the latter times and seasons of God dwelling in every part of the earth making known the signs and wonders of eternal life forming in all parts of the earth.

1

The Suffering Conditions Change by the Hands of Time

The time for better living conditions hath been already call to the people spirits reference equal living for all people are judged daily. The minds of the people balance their minds to the ways and spirits of God within them. The

God's Equal Living Conditions

suffering of the people changed in every part of the earth to the good of the people equal rights leading to eternal living. The end periods of all unrighteousness are in the last years of unequal practice in the earth. The greatest history of judgment is upon the people in the earth. The nation's leaders are over-powered with righteous spiritual minds that lead to equal rights. All things done and said in the earth are under direct spirits of righteousness toward all humankind.

All people dwelling in the earth are in the eyes of God and God's people judgment call. Are you one of God's people calling judgment in the earth on unrighteousness? All people have the right to pray for equal rights. The prayers of the people are answered quicker than ever-before

God's Equal Living Conditions

now. All people belong to God in the earth, but the unrighteous people are sifted out into judgment call by the people of God. The unrighteous people are weaned out and will not enter eternal life with the righteous people in the earth. The unrighteous traditions of the people are before judgment call of the people praying for equal rights.

The judgments and justice of God are upon the whole world of people in the world. No one escapes the latter day judgment whether good deeds or bad deeds. It is made known the eyes of God's people are in every part of the earth calling judgment on all unrighteousness. The spirits of the sovereign God almighty people are in every circumstance calling judgment and

God's Equal Living Conditions

justice to all unrighteousness. It is equally true that sins of unrighteousness lead to death. All individuals must live right to enter eternal life. All individuals must treat people equal and right in the earth so that you can live forever and never die. At the end of all sins destroyed in the earth is eternal life on a paradise earth. The direct outcome of unequal treatment from individuals is judgment call on individuals doing these things will not enter the paradise earth. There is no conflict between the spirits of God and the people because people are the spirit God within them. This means that an individual causes his or her on spiritual conflict. This means be aware of righteous spirits apart from false spirits within one's self.

God's Equal Living Conditions

The free-will to make correct choices in life that leads to eternal life on a paradise earth is the choice of all individuals. The Gospel Book of Law gives guidance to eternal life on a paradise earth. The spiritual presence of God and God's people ultimate protection are in all the earth. The traditions of humankind replace with equal rights call of judgment now in effect. What God does for one person God does for all people. All people in the earth deserve to be treated right by other people. Choose this day the righteous heart, in that you enter eternal life on a paradise earth is worth having a righteous heart. All people, places, and things have need for change at the command of God and God's people. The dwelling presence of God's people spiritual

God's Equal Living Conditions

judgment and justice prevail in all the earth. The victories of God prevail in all the earth as the people's prayers are quickly answered daily. The justice of God prevails in good or bad judgment calls with results of equal judgment call daily.

The power of God is moving on behalf of the righteous people in the earth. There is no-one that can over-step the boundaries of God's equal judgments and changes in the earth. The cleansing of the earth has already started its effect upon the people. The spirits of God's people help others make a dramatic reversal of the heart, mind, body, and soul in every area of life needed. In the mix of people, places, and things changing is eternal life on a paradise earth forever. The spiritual revelations of God's people

God's Equal Living Conditions

are in the earth gripping trouble and depression on every-side cease. The present times are different changes to the earth works itself to eternal life on a paradise earth in the anger of God's people judgments. The reign of God's promise for better economic prosperity condemns racial crude practices uncovered in equal rights to all people's judgment call. The spiritual measurements of God's righteous judgments are Holy and right spirits leading to a paradise earth. The spiritual presence of God is inside the Holy Temples and outside the Holy Temples in every place in the earth.

The spiritual victory of God has appeared in the Holy Temples in every part of the earth. The Holy people of God reign in every situation

God's Equal Living Conditions

before them. The spiritual actions of God have showed up in all the earth. The spirits of God almighty sovereign people have ordered the destruction of unrighteous spirits cease and are judged, and rejected from operating in the earth. The punishment for unequal treatment went into all the ends of the world. The consequences of unrighteous spirits stand in the earth daily before the people. The judgments of God operate in the Holy Temple and outside the Holy Temples. The royal palace of God is the Holy Temples of God. The people now focus on being Holy with righteous hearts so that they enter eternal life on a paradise earth.

The highway to heaven is built in the guidance of the Gospel Book of Law published to

God's Equal Living Conditions

all people have need of eternal life on a paradise earth. The promises of God have entered the earth in operation daily. The reconstructions of the earth continue until all unrighteous hearts and unequal treatment cease. The anointing spiritual power of the people of God is the major theme in the earth that brings peace to all humankind. The spiritual minded people have charge in the earth of judging the people hearts for righteousness in every area of life. It is God that is in control of all spiritual forces in the world. The spirits of God allow the good works of humankind that leads to eternal life and does not allow the bad works of humankind that do not lead to eternal life now operating in the earth until all unrighteous hearts cease. The good and

God's Equal Living Conditions

righteous spirits of God dwell in many people in the earth leading to all people in the earth to have righteous spirits in the world. The powerful spirits of God are irresistible spirits operating to the good of all humankind. The spiritual forces of a good effective and productive life are effective in every part of the world working to the good of the people.

It is not the importance of being a Christian, but the importance of having a righteous heart is learned from being among anointed Christian people. The frustration of the people is plain to see that God's judgment and justice is needed in every part of the earth. The Gospel Book of Law gives purchasing power for guidance to purchase eternal life on a paradise

God's Equal Living Conditions

earth. The paradise earth is eternal living without a doubt is peace and security in unity with a common bond for people treated equal. There will be no poor living conditions in the paradise earth, but all people richly live in peace without sin and death. It is the will of God new coronation of all people, places, and things that all people live richly in peace and are treated equal in a paradise heaven on earth.

The extinctions of the people spirits have reached results in one denomination created one kingdom in one Holy land for all people to become as one with the same God favoring all people. There are one faith and one religion of one big Holy land without divisions, but with permanent eternal life on a paradise earth. The

God's Equal Living Conditions

people are ready for acceptance of God's Gospel Book of Laws without contradiction and disobedience to the laws of God. The people are willing and ready to abide by the laws of God leading to a paradise heaven on earth. The signs of obedience are in the spirits of the people with special significance of righteous hearts. The rising of the people of God have predicted the fall of unrighteous hearts in every part of the earth. The people must follow God's laws as are announced in the ears of the people falling from eternal life on a paradise earth. The people become incorporated as one organized group of people in every part of the earth. The warning of God's disasters comes in many fashions changing the

God's Equal Living Conditions

earth and the spiritual minds of the people to eternal spiritual minds.

The Gospel Book of Law bears witness to the importance of spiritual minds as one and the same mind fulfilling the latter day prophecies. The religious Christian affairs are all caught up to the Holy spirits of all God's sovereign almighty powerful people. The supreme being of God's people has emerged in the earth in righteous judgment upon the people of unrighteous hearts. There are no political affairs needed in the paradise earth. The people declared God's people spirits working in every part of the earth and began to listen to God's people because there was no-other way to prevail neither enter eternal life. The massagers of God stand out in the earth spreading the renewed spirits of God leading to a paradise earth. The people submit themselves to the spirits of God and God's laws until the paradise heaven on earth appeared.

The grieved stubborn unrighteous people bear down to the spirits of God's people and become people of God's. The spirits of God do not compromise with anyone but increase righteous spirits dwelling in the earth. The Gospel Book of Law form righteous minds that are spiritually open to the ways and laws of God's eternal life. The righteous minds of the people form eternal life on a paradise earth free of sin and death. The earth is in the midst of being restored daily to accommodate eternal living. The unrighteous people are subdued by the righteous people's in the earth. Are you righteous and able to stand the seasons and times leading to eternal living? The people minds grew to recognize there are no raciest factors in heaven on earth. The words of God's people are equally swift and powerful every-where in the earth. There are many people that take charge of their lives and live righteously according to the Gospel Book of Law leading to eternal living. There are many offenses set before judgment un-forgiven. There are many offences forgiven set before the people in judgment.

The people are not to worry about false religion but allow the judgments of God to take charge. All things done and said in the earth are before the judgments and justice of God daily.

God's Equal Living Conditions

There are no-more chances left for refusal neither rejection of God's words that connect the heart to the spirits of God. The righteous ways of God are for all people in the earth. The true justice of God's people dwell till the paradise earth enters, and then there is no-more judging the people needed in eternal living. The truth and justice of God dwell daily among the people opening their conscience minds to righteous spirits. There is no-one who will disregard the laws and words of God. There are no options neither superstitious thinking reference God's laws and words. There are no oppressions from coast to coast leading to eternal life. The people must be committed without substituting obedience and making righteousness a priority in all things said and done in the earth. It is obedience to the spirits of God within you that leads you to eternal life on a paradise earth without failure. It is time to live forever and never die in heaven on a paradise earth which is eternal living.

God's Equal Living Conditions

2

Culture is the Past Conditions

The laws of God are professionally interpreted in the Gospel Book of Law so that you have clear understanding of what went into all the spirits of the earth. The spirits of God's people announce God's vengeance on the unrighteous things done in the earth daily. The need for eternal life removes sin from the heart of the people. The words "eternal life" are permanently engraved on the people's hearts. All unrighteousness surrenders to the righteous spirits of God. A stinging rebuke is pronounced against all unrighteousness. All forgiven sinners will not be punished, but must continue to live a life leading toward eternal life until the end of all sins is destroyed. The fall of unrighteous people is at the hands of righteous people's judgment. The swift return of the righteous Prophets is here in every part of the earth.

The people in the world have been declared at their darkest hours of the latter days judgment of God, people calling things as though it were and they appear in the earth. The days of entertaining angels are present as one may not

God's Equal Living Conditions

know who you are entertaining in every part of the earth. The people of God are walking in the feet and spirits of God unknown to the eyes of the unrighteous ones. The powerful spirits of God prevail among all people in the land of the living. The dead will not rise in the land of the living. The spirits of God's people unfold the minds of all unrighteous people in every area of life. The fall of all places in exile is in place at an appointed season and time of judgment call in righteous spirits in truth.

The spirits of God's people remain forever in all the earth. The wake of the people spirits comes in many different situations at hand. It is one situation will link to another situation cleansing the earth forming eternal living heaven on earth. These are the days declaring the gospel truth in the call of judgment paving the way to a paradise earth. The messages of hope for equal treatments prevail all over the world. All forgiven sinners prosper equally in the earth. The joy of the people strengthen them knowing God's people invade on the people of unrighteous spirits. The people of God put many people to shame in every part of the earth. The future days ahead take a dramatic change from the days of past and the Bible days abandon, but the gospel laws of God stand leading to eternal life.

The gospel laws are already operating spiritually in all the earth. The days call the night into place as the seasons of God's people's hands are not known by the unrighteous people. There are many things going on in the earth which quickly cease at the command of the people of God. The prompt actions of God save many people's lives unto eternal life. The reality of eternal life is forming in the midst of the people without notice to many people from generation to generation. The Queen of heaven has been revealed, heard, and seen documenting the way to eternal living. The introduction of holiness has been introduced into many religions as all religions catch up with Holiness. The mind of Holiness is a way of life leading to eternal living on a paradise earth.

Holiness went deep in all the earth forming evidence God is real within the heart, mind, body, and soul of each individual. The anointed work of God leading to eternal life is in the Holy Temples. The people of Holy Temples speak the truth leading to eternal life styles. The appointed anointed Temples are The Holiness churches of God and Christ which reign in every part of the earth. The Holy people respond to the spirits of God quickly and effectively without doubt at all times. The uncertain conditions in the earth spread quickly as the days and seasons change people, places, and things paving the way for eternal living of equal living conditions of all humankind in the earth. The change of the Bible days will be hard for many as change enter the earth. There will be no Bibles needed in the paradise earth. The Bible days will perish suddenly from the land of eternal living. It has

God's Equal Living Conditions

been unknown to many people that the Bibles of false writings cease statement saying God said things that God did not say. Many of them have added on and taken away from true Bible writings since the beginning of time. It is false bible writings have cause many deaths in the earth in every part of the world.

These things mentioned reference the Bible days are humankind committing sins from the beginning of time to brain wash the people as many have done. It is now these things change for better living have no part in eternal living. It is humankind have gotten away with words saying God said these things God did not say many statements written in Bibles. There are many people stated the Bible can-not lie. In common

God's Equal Living Conditions

sense anything written on paper can be a lie or it can be true. Many have used the Bible for monetary reasons. All false religious worship perishes in judgment call on unrighteousness in every part of the earth. It is time for all people to recognize your power is the higher power within you to work its way out of you to the good of you in righteous judgments from self-judgments.

The spirits of God's people are in the whirl-wind destroying all unrighteousness by the higher powers within them from the anointed power of God. In the course of a day many things are upon people, places, and things in the earth. There is nothing hid; all unrighteousness in the earth surfaces to the face and spirits of the righteous people calling judgment on all unrighteousness with no respect of person. The whole world is being transfigured by the forces of God's people in every area of life. The regular things of the ordinary are changing to the good of the people's equal rights. The chronological orders of all things called to happen are in force by the judgment spirits of God's people in every part of the earth. The religion of Holiness is in very powerful people in the earth called by the spirits of God calling judgment all over the earth. The powerful spirits of God's people know that God is not limited in righteous judgments in every part of the earth. The powerful actions of God's people are observed in every part of the earth. The spirits of God are deeply followed by the powerful people of God.

God's Equal Living Conditions

The spirits of God and God's people are very real in the earth. The spiritual realm of God's people is for the protection of eternal righteousness with concern for the people eternal rights. The powerful people in the earth deeply follow God's instructions clearing the way to eternal living. The astronomical prices it cost people to live are disloyal hearts imposed on those treated unequal and of misfortunes. The discoveries of unrighteous hearts are in prediction of judgment call daily. The times and seasons which fulfill judgments and justice are in the air and winds of the earth call according to the people of God's judgment call. The times are times of just judgments for all equal rights to all people in the earth. The distribution of judgment

God's Equal Living Conditions

and justice in the earth stands before all people in the earth destroying all unequal yokes.

The direct consequences of unrighteous hearts are uncovered and stripped of wrong doing near and far in the earth. The people that are lifted up high and mighty in unrighteousness are torn down in their pride is no success. The reign of the righteous people over-power the unrighteous people who are conquered in all areas of life. The people of God are committed to defending righteousness leading to eternal living. The walls of unrighteousness are torn down in disaster all around the earth as people, places, and things disappear. The days of judgment are reserved for the heart's unrighteousness. The supreme being of God's people is unknown to the eyes of the people. The psychological aspect of supreme-beings is private. God meekly leads the people's spiritual thoughts. The greatest disasters ever in history are reserved in judgments daily. The times are times to apply knowledge of eternal life toward every life style of difficult times.

The times are streaming times of periods and years of God's people's judgment in the air in every part of the earth in the justice of God. The times are high times to apply faith and confidence in all things done and said in righteousness. It is time to fix every situation in life that is to be fixed before judgment hits the situations at hand in every area of life. The things going on in unrighteousness are heart-felt in unhappiness of

God's Equal Living Conditions

many people. The firm actions of Godly spirits are daily bringing justice in many ways in the earth. The intimidation of the unrighteous has no achievements entering eternal living in the paradise earth. The times and seasons force everyone dwelling in the earth to acknowledge the presence of God and God's people's spirits dwelling in the earth accomplishing eternal purposes. The presence of God's spirits and God's people's spirits dwelling in the earth daily measure the spirits of humankind for righteousness in every part of the earth. .

    The changes called in the earth by God and God's people daily measure standards recognizing need for change evolving around the unrighteous hearts of the people. The people

God's Equal Living Conditions

treated unfairly in the earth have need for change leading to eternal living. The call of full measurements of judgment and justice dwells among all people in the earth. All people in the earth are to engage in equal treatment of others.

3

The People Are Guaranteed Equal Rights

The Holy Priest closely leads the people to the links of the Holy spirits of God. The people in the earth are closely led to all directions of equal rights raised in every part of the earth. The people in every part of the earth now comprehend the powerful works of God working through the people of God. The fullness of God's spirits and God's people's spirits are over all the earth referring to the Gospel book of law. The people in the earth face realness of God and God's people judgment call and justice. The people who had lost sight of the words and spirits of God are brought back to reality in spirits of God. The spirits of God and God's people warn the people they are judged daily in all things said and done in all parts of the earth. These are the chosen days of God's judgments and justice upon the people. The judgments and justice of God and God's people are without count in numbers daily in the earth.

God's Equal Living Conditions

The times and seasons are now God and God's people denounced judgments and justice on all false social religious corruptions in the earth. The spirits of God said be ye Holy in the earth for I God am Holy in all the earth among the people in Holy spirits in truth. The Prophet had written the Gospel Book of Law according to the spirits of God's thresh-hold over every mind in the universe. The spirits of God and God's people will demolish all religions except Holiness religion in all the earth. There will be no other religion to enter the Holy land except Holiness religion called by the spirits of God and God's people. The punishment and suffering of the people in the air over all the earth are the judgments and justice of God and God's people for those who refuse eternal living on a paradise earth. There will be no false religions to enter the paradise earth.

There are no Bible scriptures needed in the paradise earth because the earth cleanness prevails. The people quickly seek Holiness over all the earth leaving false religions of corrupt sanctuaries formed for the purpose of monetary reasons and not to the saving of souls unto eternal life. The souls of the people must be saved unto Holiness for the purpose of eternal life of eternal living. The true standards of Holy religions of God and God's people prevail over all false religions in the earth.

The true Holy gospel structures of God and God's people prevail and reform the earth to a paradise land of eternal living saving the lives of

God's Equal Living Conditions

the people. The Holy judgments and justice of God and God's people prevail in all the earth. The people in all the earth must live right under Holiness structure of Holy Temple to wisely enter eternal life over all the earth. The righteous structured conducts of all the people enter eternal living on a paradise earth with heaven on earth as soon as every conduct prevails over the earth. The latter-days of God and God's people prevail over corrupt minds that make no connection with the spirits of God. The latter-days of God and God's people wipe-out all unrighteous with judgments and justice spirits in all the earth. The only stages of prosperous days are for the unrighteous to enter faith with righteous Holy minds. There is no Holy Temple without Holy

God's Equal Living Conditions

Prophets in the Holy Temple to make the connections to the minds of the people needed with God called by the spirits of God.

The righteous conducts of the people are the righteous blessings of the people seeing their enemies destroyed in every part of the earth. The transfigurations of God and God's people have transported spirits all over the earth in judgments and justice for prosperous equal rights that destroy the ways of the unrighteous people. There are no conflicts between the messages of God and God's people referenced in the written Gospel Book of Law called by the spirits of God. The judgments and justice of God are not delayed, but already prevail in the earth measuring the people by a righteous straight-line.

God's Equal Living Conditions

The authority of God and God's people is already operating in Holiness, in righteousness, and in cleansing the earth of unrighteousness with all mighty powerful spirits from God. There are no confrontations in Holy Temples neither in Holy spirits; any that awakens confrontations will see the judgments and justice of God suddenly and quickly in every part of the earth.

    Judgments and justice are operating in the spirits of God and God's people; all things dwelling in the earth not equally prosperous for the people are destroyed along with its maker. The notice of judgments and justice has been served on all people, places, and things said and done in the earth that are unrighteous. Are you one of the unrighteous people? All people, places, and things in the earth are weighted on equal rights and change where needed in the judgments and justice of God and God's people. The judgments of God and God's people are timeless in seasons and out of seasons. The judgments and justice of God and God's people are un-escapable upon all nations in the earth. The judgments and justice of God and God's people are magnified upon all people spread equal righteousness of God.

The downfall of many people is sin committed over and over without fail. There is failure in the unrighteous minds leading to death. The strongholds of the unrighteous mind raid the conscious of the righteous mind. The approach of unrighteousness is overturned and cease in every part of the earth. The wicked are invaded by the spirits of God and God's people. All sinful ways disappear from the people in the earth. The prosperous ways of God and God's people are not limited. All people are welcome to eternal living with righteous hearts on a paradise earth where there won't be a need for the Bible because all people are righteous and holy. These messages to the people are the powerful spiritual writing of the Prophet from the spirits of God and God's people in the earth. These powerful messages in this book are mentioned in every part of the earth. These messages are powerful tools to live by reaching eternal living on a paradise heaven on earth. The spiritual messages in this book which contain no doubt and extend beyond human

God's Equal Living Conditions

thinking, lead to ways of God and God's people. The supreme spiritual being of God and God's people dwells in the earth physically and mentally.

There is much focus and attention placed on the resurrection of God and God's people's spirits operating in the earth within the Gospel Book of Law. The people are encouraged by the words of these spiritual messages written by the Prophet's spirits of God within her. The messages of the Prophet's walking and spiritual writing in the earth change the minds of the people according to the purpose of God and God's people. The messages are for the inspiration of the people to obey God's words and instructions leading to eternal life on a paradise earth. The

God's Equal Living Conditions

highest Priest Prophet ever to walk the foundations of the earth in your time speaks to you according to the spirits of God and God's people in the earth, that ye change your ways of death for eternal living and never die.

The equal rights of the people are released to them in all the earth as sins of the unrighteous perish from the earth. The joyful arrival of God and God's people's judgments and justice of equal rights pleases the people and is received by the people in every part of the earth. The careless leaders in leadership have a change of mind and want to live eternal life and treat the people with equal rights in righteousness. The people in leadership do not want to be condemned by God and God's people in every

God's Equal Living Conditions

part of the earth. The spirits of God have already strengthened the people against the unrighteousness of equal rights. There are wonderful days to come from the labor of the righteous. The future for the people is eternal life on an eternal earth. The present times are clearing up the way to a paradise eternal earth. The powerful spirits of God and God's people renew refresh spirits that remove everything in the earth that offends the people. It is the now times and seasons that God and God's people have appeared giving the people with forgiven sins spiritual minds to live eternal life.

    All people in the earth have sinned and come short of receiving the righteous spirits of the coming of God within the people of God in

God's Equal Living Conditions

every part of the earth. The whole world is God's kingdom of heaven on earth. The unrighteous things done in the earth become scarce forming the way to eternal living. The poor living conditions of the people are removed from the earth within the perishing of unrighteousness. The people of God, who set the ways of God in every part of the earth, are the Holy chosen people of God. The Holy people of God dwell in the Holy Temples of God. The churches of God and Christ are the appointed of Temples of God to lead the way to eternal life. The respect of Good people has the peace of God within their heart. It is the good and righteous hearts of the people following the structured ways of God and God's people to eternal living.

God's Equal Living Conditions

The Holy gospel is a true religion as all else fails in the eye sight of God and God's people. The people and their family daily livings are in the eye sight of God and God's people. The cares of God and God's people strengthen the people into wanting to do the things required for eternal living. The relationships of daily living faithful and true to each other in the earth are a requirement to enter eternal life. The Holy religions attract and attack the people who want to live eternal life. All standards of God and God's people are lifted up in the earth. All people in the earth approve of each other. Cult ministry relationships fail to enter eternal life on a paradise earth. God is actively charging all ministries not to mislead the people. All people in the earth must reflect on the

God's Equal Living Conditions

spirits of God and God's people that are now before them. The people reflect on racial religious groups that attract certain cultural relationships. The reality of God is upon all sin committed in the name of God by many ministries. It is now without parallel one cannot escape the latter day anger of God and God's people in every part of the earth. It is the times and seasons of now, that God requires the people to rise up a standard in love.

The earth is turning into a peaceful loving place without racial wickedness. All good spirits within the people, all places, and all things in the earth belong to God and God's people. The equal justice of God and God's people roam the earth daily. The equal rights of the people are in the air

God's Equal Living Conditions

spiritually fixing all people, places, and things earthly. The unfair treatments of the people have roamed the earth long enough to cease are called by the spirits of God and God's people. There are no more wars and rumors of wars after the latter day's judgments are over. God and God's people will have fulfilled all purposes in the earth that are to be fulfilled with equality and love for each other.

I, the Lord and the people of God, have looked around and seen the unfair treatment and equal rights violated upon the people. All amounts of evil wickedness imposed on the people cease in judgment and justice earthly. The daily deeds of the people are before the judgments and justice of God and God's people

God's Equal Living Conditions

daily giving an account of unrighteousness impose on the people. The condemning situations of the people are at hand in judgments of those who know who they are. The spirits of the Lord and the Lord's people said the time and seasons are up for unequally yoked relationships.

God's Equal Living Conditions

4

The End of Stressful Times

Surface

The unrighteousness of the people has held the people down long enough with rules that regulate many equal rights taken from the people. I, the Lord, say to you search your hearts without fail and do what is right in the eye sight

God's Equal Living Conditions

of God and God's people. The rebuilding of the people's minds has already spiritually started. The spiritual feeding of the people that believe in God and God's people is written in the Gospel Book of Law. The promise of God's people's prosperity is now here forming in the earth daily.

The standards of God and God's people are set standards the people have need of. The starting point of every situation has formed for the good of the struggle of the people in the economic hardship. The persistence of God is in all things promised unto the people who faint not. The vision word God is written on the people's forehead God's people visible to the chosen elect people of God calling judgments. The spirits of God are powerfully used by the people of God. The restoring of the people has already been set in the earth operating daily in all things said and done. The acceptable times and seasons of holiness in the earth are now times increasing as God and God's people receive the people of God for the paradise earth. The people are now in the mind set to turn away from wrong doing in the earth. It is from the beginning of time God said be Holy for I am Holy in all things said and done. There are no people in the earth who disregard the words of God and God's people. The spirits of God are called to all people in the earth. The seasons and times are just right for some and too late for others.

    The spirits of the people are renewed from stressful times as the people change from

God's Equal Living Conditions

last to first in all things said and done in the earth. The Lord and the Lord's people have equal rights among the people. The broken hearts are healing forming new ages of seasons and times. The people of God look forward to the new times and seasons as the people reconcile with one-another ending all crisis of unequal rights. The promising times of God have sent one last Prophet to lead the way to eternal life. The coming of the Prophet God sent is in the latter days of the Messiah has come within the Prophet's spirits. The Prophet is the Prophet of the Highest to ever walk the foundations of the earth in the now times of judgment call for eternal life on a paradise earth. There will never be another to come as the paradise earth forms daily. There is no need for another coming because the people in the earth will be perfect. The honors and wisdom of the Highest Priest Prophet without fail have risen. It is the now times and seasons all things are called by God and God's people formed in the earth quickly without fail and without void.

The Christians everywhere agree that many Christians have tried to live by many Bible standards but fail in their trying. In the paradise earth are all perfect people without fail. There are many scriptures in the Bible that words were added and words were taken from the scriptures by many false writers that called themselves inspired by God, but they were not inspired by God. There were many writers of reprobated minds. God had turned them over to their reprobated minds. These things from the beginning of times and seasons brought sins and God's judgments into the world upon all people born into a world of sinful reprobated minds of many people. The present times of sins are replayed of the people's forefathers who appointed rules to their families passed from generation to generation. The judgments of God are upon all people, places, and things in the earth of humankind and include all religious writings of Bibles and religious books.

This very day God did not say things people have said God spoke to them. The times are now times God is not a store front for money. The spiritual judgments of God and God's people are upon the use of God's name for money

God's Equal Living Conditions

purposes. These are the times of the Highest Priest Prophet is here that has ever walked the foundations of the earth in your times and seasons. Jesus was the Highest Priest Prophet called by the spirits of God as God told Jesus to write all things spoken to him and go tell the people what I the Lord your God have spoken to you in spirits in truth. The same as God has spoken to the Highest Priest Prophet to ever walk the earth in your times and seasons of now times. The Bible was written for the people to have instructions to follow, but many people of the Bible days added words and took words from what God said to their spirits, that why the Bible is so confusing to many people in the world today.

God's Equal Living Conditions

The time is now times and seasons. I God say to you do not worry a lot about what has been written that you do not understand as much as making your own heart right with righteous spirits within you. I, the Lord, bring you more understanding than ever before leading you to a perfect world of people beginning now in your times and seasons of now times. There are no more confusions as times before as you a people allow righteous spirits to work in your heart with righteous actions and activities. In the past times Jesus tried to please the people and the people were not pleased with Jesus. There are many people that have become pleased with Jesus today looking and watching for the return of Jesus. There has not been any attempt on the part of Jesus to return. The dead turn to dust in the earth with no return. It is time to put sense with things that are happening in everyday life.

There are many people in the earth who are not pleased with the written lies of the people. It is time to make a connection with the truth within reasonable things happening around you. There is no one can figure out why the dead has not risen and why Jesus has not made an attempt to return to earth. There are no dead bodies alive talking of returning to earth. Does this make sense to you? It is time to face reality of the real world in judgment being guided toward a paradise eternal earth. In the Bible days the people called Jesus a liar and told Jesus God had given them scriptures to write. It was then Jesus

God's Equal Living Conditions

allowed the people to take part in writing the Bible with Him. This is when the confusion started in some scriptures and has led many people to confusion as of this very day. This is why the disciples and Jesus and people of the past with no return to earth.

The judgments of God were upon them with eternal death. The death of people is eternal death. The people who live until eternal earth is finished have eternal life and never die. The death of people has always been eternal death. It is in this very day God has allowed the people to operate the earth within their reprobated minds. It is now times and seasons God and God's people are calling judgment against all reprobated minds in the earth. The reprobated minds of the people operating the earth made sins grow stronger and stronger in every part of the earth. The reprobated minds of humankind strayed from the righteous spirits of God to their own money making spirits using God's name for money purposes. The stressful minds of the people cease with time and seasons forming a paradise earth.

The times and seasons are now forming eternal life in the earth that has been called by God and God's people. The people of the past in the Bible days had eternal life on earth until Jesus allowed them to take part in the Bible writings of many scriptures that confused many people of the past and now days cause the people to sin causing eternal death. It was in the Bible days God rejected the people for disobeying the laws and commands of God. There are many true scriptures in the Bible as there are many untrue scriptures in the Bible. The spirits of the Lord God said be wise in your own thinking that leads to eternal life with heaven on earth a paradise earth. The times and seasons of latter days judgment and disaster are upon the mouths of the people without knowledge of God's mysterious ways and spirits. The stressful Bible arguments are now stopped; ceased in every part of the earth. The argument of being unsure is the time to be quiet and wait on the Lord your God and God's people and see what happens with what has been written unto you. It is time to go by the actions of words that have been written rather than words alone. The words written without actions are

God's Equal Living Conditions

dead words written to you. The written dead words of people cease with judgments seasons and time.

The real words written that are true lead to eternal life on a paradise earth. It is times and seasons to recognize people of God with powerful spirits operating in the earth with authority belonging to God. The hidden mysteries of wisdom and knowledge of God and God's people are powerful issues with many people in the earth. It is times and seasons to be led to eternal living or you will be misled to eternal death. There are people in the earth without count who have faithful spirits of God from the powers of God's spirits who are ready and willing to lead the people toward eternal life. The purpose of recognizing the powerful people in the earth with powerful spirits is the unfolding of the paradise earth forming through these people. The minds of the people have been scared and distracted from the spiritual truth of eternal living. The false ways of living fades from the mind of the people living in ways that cause disaster.

It is time to practice living developed renewed skills of eternal living in every part of the earth. The interest of eternal living wise is daily focus with quality living and equal living keeping in mind you are being judged for unfair treatment of others. The clearing of the earth of sins is in progress daily dwelling in the earth. The redesign of the earth is forming daily to the good of the people eternal living. It is times and seasons for

God's Equal Living Conditions

the people to pray that you comprehend all things said and done leading to eternal living. The people must value your spirits leading to eternal living with a faithful heart and understanding. The accuracy of eternal life must be viewed and remembered in a moralized set of beliefs within your spirit. The times and seasons are bursting at the scenes with eternal living as the sands of the sea without count are eternal deaths at the blink of an eye. The freedom and equal rights of all people living in the earth prevail with all unrighteous hearts swallowed up in eternal death. The things in the people's spirits that are unbecoming to eternal living are cast from the spirits of the people in every part of the earth.

God's Equal Living Conditions

The historical view of false literature ceases from roaming the earth affecting the minds of the people. The people with clean hearts treat people equally right leading to eternal living heaven on earth. The written predictions written unto you belong to spirits of God given to the spirits of the writer. The spirits of the writer, which come from God, come true, and then you know they are true spirits from God. All things written before you stand before God's judgment at this very hour until the paradise earth appear. There is no special category of people dwelling in the paradise earth, but all things done and said receive judgment daily until the paradise earth appears. It is at the command of God and God's people the renewing of the earth appears daily

God's Equal Living Conditions

until eternal living finishes its course. The renewing of the earth prepares for the paradise earth for all people to perform one and the same. The spirits in the earth have independent thinking ability aware that God's spirits can allow and disallow controlling all spirits in the air. The good future spirits hold the key to reviving the earth to eternal living.

God's Equal Living Conditions

5

The Outbreak of God's Power

The spirits of God's authority have already been reaffirmed in the earth in spirits in truth. The people are under the authority of controlled spirits of God and God's people. The deep powerful spirits of God and God's people are standing deep in the earth with honorific powerful authority in every part of the earth. The

God's Equal Living Conditions

people are called to repentance to enter eternal spirits for eternal living. The standing of eternal spirits is in every part of the earth. The people have need of knowing how to receive eternal life in heaven which is on earth. I, the Lord, God says to you be not confounded by your own thoughts in speech in heart and body. It is time to stop living in vain and find out the eternal living ways of God. The living ways of God are not like the living ways of mankind. The comfort of knowing the blessed ways of God's judgments upon the people isn't treating the people unequal. The people live according to the purpose of God's eternal living.

There are no discriminations among the people of clean hearts. The nationality of people

God's Equal Living Conditions

is not the importance of eternal life but the spiritual heart and actions. The stressful past is the past and the eternal future is the future. The importance to life is eternal living on a paradise earth. The past traditions of the people will no-longer stress the people with unfair treatments. The people of God share in preparing ways of eternal living within the spirits of the people. The people must reason with the true spirits of God within their heart where there are new discoveries. The days of God are obvious facts that all humankind reaches eternal living. The truth as never before dwells before all humankind in the earth reference eternal living on a paradise earth. The information of eternal life now before you is for the purpose and knowledge of eternal

God's Equal Living Conditions

living. The arrival of God's new spirits is affecting the people successfully. These are the days of God's equal judgments and justice in the earth. The gospel book of God's laws strongly influences the important facts of living eternal life. The message from God's reference to eternal life is accurately stated and written for the remembrance of taking action to inherit eternal living. The signs dwelling in the earth are renewed gospel religious ministries leading to eternal living which is significant to all people dwelling in righteousness. The signs of the times, seasons, and change of all people, places, and things said and done in the earth are changing to the good of the people receiving eternal life.

God's Equal Living Conditions

The spirits of God and God's people's knowledge roam the earth making changes where needed in all things said and done in every part of the earth. The increase of righteous spiritual living appears over the entire earth. The equal rights of all people appear in the hearts of world leaders to treat all people with equal living and providing ways everyone can live according to God's standards for eternal living. The judgments of God and God's people's spirits are in the winds blown all over the earth instantly spreading righteous spirits of eternal equal living in the minds of all world leaders being judged for eternal life on a paradise earth. The increasing serious gospel ministries in the earth are recognized in all Holy ministries. The justice of God and God's people

God's Equal Living Conditions

prevails in every part of the earth daily. The guidance of Holy Christians leads the people to eternal life on a paradise earth. There will be many people converted to Holy gospel for the chance to receive eternal life and never die on a paradise earth.

The proper order of all people, places, and things falls into place according to the spirits of the righteous hearts called by the spirits of God and God's people. The chronological order of events is plainly happening in the earth reaching the age of eternal life in eternal living on a paradise earth. The people in the earth witness the Holy Priest guiding the people to eternal living on a paradise earth. The testimonies of the people get stronger and stronger. The good news

God's Equal Living Conditions

to all people dwelling in the earth is eternal living is in the process of world changes to the good of the people. The people must be patient, believe, have forgiven sins, and righteous in heart in order to receive eternal life on a paradise earth without sinful hearts. The resurrection of righteous spirits of world leaders in the earth must show the people are being served with equal living. There are many Holy men and women ministering to the people in the society of Holy living. The signs of the destruction of the unrighteous hearts as unworthy to receive eternal life are seen having many troubles in every part of the earth where they see their judgment of God and God's people.

The judgment call and justice of God and God's people have showed up throughout the

God's Equal Living Conditions

world spreading warnings of God's destruction upon the people and world leadership. The world leaders in leadership have a need to create equal rights for all people under their leadership. The judgment and justice of equal living conditions are in judgment daily. The hopeless living conditions cease in the over-haul of God and God's people's judgment call. The success of the people is at the heart eternal living on a paradise earth. The judgmental attitudes for greed cease and gear toward helping the people flow and stream in living in proper conditions. The mention of God and God's people calling judgments and justice in the earth give way to wise thinking and righteous hearts to treat all humankind equally with food and living conditions. The Holy Spirit intervenes in everyone's spirits dwelling in the earth

There are more accurate activity and power among the people of God. The evidence of God and God's people's powerful spirits points to the world's sins now falling by methods of God and God's people's judgments and justice called upon the people. The violence in the world ceases from the minds of the people when they are created equal in a world of unfair treatment with no justice in sight. The just judgments of God and God's people bring many changes to a dying world of people. The people of God have a special relationship with God. The people of the Holy Temples recognize God and God's people's spirits operating in the earth. The spirits of God and

God's Equal Living Conditions

God's people's are inflicted on the people's spirits leading them to eternal life on a paradise earth of heavenly living. The messages of God and God's people are confirmed through reality of God and God's people's judgments in the earth.

The social formalities of judgments and justice are made known in every part of the earth forming eternal living in the depths of the earth. The Holy Priest teaches the people about eternal life on a paradise earth. The call of God is equal rights in future living standards in every part of the earth appear. The social living of all people showing love toward one-another appears. The violence of guns disappears as guns are swallowed up in the grounds of the earth. The trust and love for future living prevail over

God's Equal Living Conditions

violence. The greatness of God and God's people are all around the earth bringing out distinctive facts of eternal life and the judgments and justice of equal living conditions. The times and seasons for judgment of the unfaithfulness of hypocrites in the world are called up front and judged to cease in every part of the earth. There will be no-one in the earth to play on the minds of the people. The revelation in the earth is all humankind speaks the truth with fairness of equal systematic accounts of equal living.

The judgments of God and God's people denounce all unrighteousness which ceases in the earth. There are no false religions neither false teachings for the purpose of leadership wealth cease in all parts of the earth. The emphases of

God's Equal Living Conditions

eternal living spirits of God and God's people are upon the people in judgment and justice rejecting unrighteous spirits in the earth. There are no misunderstandings of the Holy Gospel called of God and God's Holy people. The reconstruction of the gospel calls for the people to be as one and the same in the eye sight of God and God's people's judgment. The presence of God and God's people prevails. In the earth prevail. The judgment of sinful ways of men, women, and children is in the eye sight of God and God's people. The people of God's spirits are one and the same is God in the earth. The spirits of God and God's people immediately overpowered all unrighteous spirits of people in the earth daily.

God's Equal Living Conditions

The dwelling spirits in the earth are messages from God and God's people in the earth saying all people, places, and things said and done in the earth are before us in judgment and justice daily as eternal life appears. The future days of God and God's people's spirits rule in the earth. The good news of God and God's people's justice and judgment overpower all wickedness of unrighteousness in the earth. The people of God respond to the spirits of God within them, the gift of God's judgments. The contents of Holiness are in all the earth seeking spiritual righteousness of equal rights of eternal living conditions. The Holiness disciples of God, appearing in all the earth, are over all the earth's judgment and justice call. There is renewed confidence in the

God's Equal Living Conditions

people referenced by the Holy disciple people of God. The spiritual resurrection of God and God's disciples are in all the earth more than ever before. The empty minds of the people in the earth are resurrected from dead minds to spiritual minds alive in the earth. The spirits of God and God's people said to the spirits of the people this world will never end.

6

Victory appears with Heaven on Earth

The life of eternal living is given to the chosen people of God who endure until the end of all sins on earth. The heavens forming on earth bring change to all individuals on earth. The spirits of God and God's people peel off the

God's Equal Living Conditions

interpretation of all misunderstanding of scriptures written and rewritten many times for the purpose of wealthy leadership. The historical living of eternal life in heaven is forming on earth as the minds of the people seek eternal living from the Holy Temples. The force of God's and God's people spirits are upon on the people forcing them to make a choice of eternal living, knowing that death is eternal. The readers of the words of God are forced to comprehend and make a decision to follow God and God's people's eternal purpose for humankind. It is God's purpose that no soul be lost to eternal death. The purpose of God and God's people is that all people have claim on eternal living heaven on a paradise earth free from sin.

God's Equal Living Conditions

The special emphasis is on all people having a need to claim eternal living among all humankind. The prediction of God and God's disciples' resurrection is here in the heavens placed on earth. It is the now times of God here on earth in the spiritual body of the spiritual disciple people of God. The world documentation of world domination is changing by the spiritual words of God and God's people seeking equal eternal living on a paradise earth. There is no politic religion in the earth called by the spirits of God and God's people. The world wide Holy gospel of God and God's people is to teach the people how to receive eternal life on a paradise earth. The famous sermon is "God and God's people are in the earth and have always been in

God's Equal Living Conditions

the earth awaiting such times as these of today in judgment and justice. The Holy appointed Churches of God in Christ take charge of judgmental spirits in the earth called by the spirits of God. The link between the old and the new spirits in the earth is the new spirits are eternal spirits referring to eternal living on a paradise earth with equal living conditions for all people living in the earth forming into a paradise earth.

The link appeared between humankind and God's spirits within humankind attributing honor to all who believe in their own spirits within them belonging to the God head of all people, places, and things on earth forming into eternal living. The Holy commissioned saints are the appointed chosen ones judge the people for

God's Equal Living Conditions

eternal living. The Heirs of God are the Holy people of God called according to God's purpose for eternal life. The success of God and God's people is understood as the spiritual mind of the people operates in togetherness forming eternal living equally and righteously. The birth of eternal living is daily formed in the minds of the people. The times are now times to repent from using Gods name for the purpose of money wealth. The times are now times to repent from misleading the people. The times are now times for each individual to take responsibility for sins committed accepting righteous spirits choosing to be chosen people of God. It is now times to follow the Holy chosen people of God to eternal living.

God's Equal Living Conditions

The call of all Holy Priest has a great reward of eternal life on a paradise earth. The Holy Priest has power to feed the people with the words of God which gives eternal life on a paradise earth without sin. The times are now times of righteous spirits in truth in judgment daily. The times are now times for religious spiritual immatureness to cease. The times are now times of whatever goes on deep in the minds of the people must be spiritual minded. The times are now times and seasons of no other religions left standing but Holiness leading to eternal life on a paradise earth. The warnings against false religions are deep in the earth judging the motives, thoughts, and intentions of the people with thoughts other than a Holy land. The forming

God's Equal Living Conditions

of one big Holy land is already in the forces of the air formed by the spirits of God and God's holy people. The spiritual things of God and God's people have taken root in the earth. The instructions and warnings of God and God's people are saying do not be harsh to others, but be fair and equal in all things. The people must decide what first priorities in life are and put spirits of God first that leads to eternal life living on a paradise earth. There will be no discriminating against others, but treat others the way you want to be treated with or without money.

    The times are now times to make sure you are on the right track to eternal living on the right path in all things said and done daily. The times

God's Equal Living Conditions

are now times to be careful that you do not mislead others in things you say and do. The times are now times to make good decisions and not deceive others. The right paths are taught by the Holy people of God that are very spiritual minded in all things said and done. These are now times all humankind abides by the spirits of God and God's people renewing the spiritual minds of the people into eternal living on a heavenly paradise earth. The people are required to live in the path of eternal living without sinful hearts. The Gospel Book of law guides the people into eternal living on a paradise earth. It is good to remember that the spirits of God and God's people are watching all things said and done in the earth daily in eternal judgments and justice.

God's Equal Living Conditions

The laws of God are called to all nations of people according to the Gospel Book of Law. The focus of God and God's people is the restoring of the people's sanity mentally and physically in the earth. The form of new expressions and comments of older people and young people is to respect each other's feelings making corrections where needed. The times are now to avoid giving one-another wrong ideas, remembering all things said and done daily are in spiritual judgments' of God and God's people. The times are now, times to spread the good news is reference to eternal living and eternal life on a paradise heaven on earth. The Holy Priest and Holy Prophets have instructions on how to guide the people into eternal living on a paradise earth. The Holy Priest

God's Equal Living Conditions

and Holy Prophets have spiritual power from on high according to God's Holy spirits. The Holy Prophets and Holy Priest are spiritually motivated to guide the people into eternal living. There is no fear in God and God's people's progression toward eternal living.

The people of God are in the will of God's eternal spirits. The people have been worn down spiritually by the burden of not having equal rights within equal living conditions. These things cease in all the earth according to the Gospel Book of Law and the spirits of God and God's people. The spirits of unequal treatment which have been inflicted on the people cease in all nations. These are the powerful seasons and now times that the standards of eternal living prevail

God's Equal Living Conditions

in the earth daily. The stubborn hearts that deny the spirits in the earth belong to God, and God's people can't enter eternal living in denial of true spirits. These things stand in judgments of God and God's people daily. The times are now times dwelling in the earth are spectacular signs of God and God's people's spirits which are resurrected in all the earth in values of true judgments and justice.

The righteous and the unrighteous all stand before God and God's people's spirits in judgments and justice. The judgments of God and God's people are for entering the Kingdom of eternal life with heaven on earth. The kingdom at heaven is at hand forming in all the earth. It is never too late to have a change of heart to do

God's Equal Living Conditions

well. The gospel messages of God's kingdom forming in the earth now exist. The dominion of God and God's people's power exists in authority in spirits in truth. The reign of God and God's people is active in the earth. The kingdom of God has been revealed to the Holy Prophets and the Holy Priest. The seasons and times reveal to all humankind the revelation times of the kingdom forming in the earth. The acknowledgement of the kingdom of God and God's people is forming heaven on earth. There will be no more conflicts with traditional ways of humankind, for traditions phased out have already been denounced as water under the bridge. The understanding of true Holiness occurs when the future fulfills the true gospel laws of God's eternal living.

God's Equal Living Conditions

The living reality is evidence of things seen and hoped for fulfilled by the spiritual authority of God and God's people. The spiritual authority of God and God's people rules in the earth. The seasons and times are now times of spiritual obedience demanded by the spirits of God and God's people. The supreme value of spiritual authority rules in all things said and done. The value of clean hearts and clean hands has a great weight on the judgment of eternal life. There will be no different standards in religion, but one and the same Holy religion. The kingdom of God's people will operate totally in a spiritual mind set. There will be no contrary teaching other than Holiness in every effort made to save the people to inherit eternal life. The people of all nations

God's Equal Living Conditions

must live spiritual minded to be forgiven of their sins individually.

The life of eternal living on a paradise earth is for all people who have forgiven sins among them. The people of eternal life have the word God written on their forehead visible to the spiritual - minded people judging the people. The chosen people of God look forward to joyous days ahead in the kingdom of God's heaven on earth. The judgments and justice of God and God's people are in control of the spirits leading to eternal life on a paradise earth. The expectation of a new world order is forming the resurrection of eternal living. The apocalyptic movement within the revelation movement flourishes within spiritual order called by the spirits of God and

God's Equal Living Conditions

God's people. The Supreme Being is the spiritual leaders walking the foundations of the earth call a thing as though it was and it be in the earth. The spirits of God and God's people crush all oppositions of unequal living. The new blessed order of things is forming as the faithful people with good hearts are released from oppression. The glory of eternal life reigns creating a paradise heaven on earth.

The beautiful Holy gates of God's doors are at the Holy Temples of God where men, women, and children attend for guidance into eternal life and never die. The Holy people at the Holy temples dwell in spirits of true hope forming eternal lives. The ordinary symbolic vision of a paradise earth forms heaven on earth in reality.

God's Equal Living Conditions

The visions of apocalypse among the people exist within the judgments and justice of God and God's people called of judgment upon the people. The Holy disciples of God returning to do the work God have called them to do above all great warriors are the people of God on a mission. The victories of real hope are uttered by God and God's people in the earth. The independence of God's people's spirits is stirred up for the equal living rights of the people entering a paradise earth. The equal rights of all people, places, and things are brought to the light of the people. The people have a need to live equally on a paradise earth. The kingdom of God and God's people unites in the consolidation of equal living conditions in judgment for the people. The economy depression of the people ceases in every part of the earth. The break-down of equal justice are called forth in the spirits of the people in judgment.

God's Equal Living Conditions

7

All spirits of the People United

The spirits of equal justice spread around the earth in judgments and justice of God and God's people. The spiritual dispersing of a conservative spiritual atmosphere of a distinctive way of living eternal life has entered the spirits of the people in the earth. The people's spirits are saying there is no need for unclean food in a

God's Equal Living Conditions

paradise earth. The unclean unhealthy food that is not good for the people ceases in the earth. The drastic steps taken to fulfill the commitment of better living conditions on a paradise earth are in judgment until the better living conditions appear in the earth. The people in the earth fear the devouring spirits of God and God's people's judgments over-looking the earth in the set seals of judgment and justice. The powerful authority of God and God's people's spirits detour all false religions that are not Holy Temples saving the lives of the people. The inspired devotional choir members of the Holy Temples save many people by opening up their spiritual hearts in faith in truth.

God's Equal Living Conditions

The bursting out of eternal life is in the earth with full actions seen and heard within the marvelous things said and done cutting the customs and traditions of the people. The bursting out of eternal life cuts all rough edges moving swiftly through the earth with resurrecting frame work beyond the imagination of the people. The occurring actions of many things happening in the earth is the call of God and God's people making clear the way to eternal living on a paradise earth. The heavens dwelling on earth and appearing in every part of the earth are pure and clean hearts geared toward living eternal life. The people are in close touch with God's spirits leading them to the luxury of eternal life.

God's Equal Living Conditions

The spiritual discernment of all religious leaders comprehends the ways of God's spiritual forces in the earth. The spiritual order first is Prophets second are Priests and third are Evangelists in ranks. The greatest appearance is the coming of the greatest Prophet of your time here in the earth, the fulfillment of the spirit of the Messiah on earth. The Holy gospel's purpose is saving the people who enter eternal life and never die. The written evidence introduces the spirits of God to the people describing the gospel book of law. These are the days of spiritual call of God and God's people prevail. The long year of praying is over, and now is the judgment and justice call, the answer to the prayers of the people. The many situations in the earth are the

God's Equal Living Conditions

purpose of God and God's people cleansing the earth.

The call of judgment has opened the earth to the natural forces of God and God's people's spiritual judgment and justice over all the earth. The unholy priesthood for the purpose of wealth is attacked by spiritual forces of judgment and brought to failure. The true interpretation of God's judgment on earth is the factual things happening around the earth. The intervention of God's powerful Prophet utters judgments and justice upon the troublesome times of destruction in the earth. The spiritual forces of judgments cure the troublesome times of the people. The powerful word of the greatest Prophet who has walked the earth in your times

God's Equal Living Conditions

has a great influence on the powerful spirits of God's people's judgments in the earth.

The events of God and God's people's prayers are being answered surprisingly over all the earth. The judgments of God and God's people are being revealed through times of increased predictions of the future. The times and seasons have already brought about events that were already in the call of judgment prior to times and seasons of now times. The increase of many accidental deaths in many places is the essence of time and judgments. The call of a paradise earth of God and God's people's prayers is being answered in many ways that have to surface to clear the way for heaven on earth. The specified times and places of God and God's people's judgments are in the plain spiritual forces in the earth. The messages of God and God's people's judgments are real in the earth with much force all over the earth from coast to coast. The just judgmental spirits of God and God's people dwell according to the unrighteous spirits of the people in the earth.

The victory of just judgment brings obedience and faith in the life of the people in the call of spiritual obedience. The echoes of the powerful spirits of the powerful Prophets reach the spiritual ears of God's people. The powerful Prophet like in the days of Jesus has risen up by the supreme spiritual powers of God. The succeeding identical ways of the powerful Prophet are identical to the ways of Jesus who

God's Equal Living Conditions

was a Prophet in the Bible days. The prophetic judgments echoed clearly shows God and God's people's judgments operating in the earth it is the spirits of God which permit the good and the bad events to clear the way to the paradise earth. There are many blessings on the way from the many events of good and bad events happening around the world. The blessings of God come through individual spiritual obedience that dwells within you daily through the relationship of God's spirits.

The judgment call in the earth distinctively planted the good and the bad to clear the way to eternal life from a sinful people in the earth. The provision of an evil corrupt system of practice is in failure of influencing others. The signs of

God's Equal Living Conditions

trouble for those in authority already exist in favoritism in failure. The unrighteous hearts are not a threat to the righteous hearts. The idle threats are in high places of subservices of high cost to live or be added to group of people, places, and things. The treacherous disloyal services to the unfortunate are in failure. The visions and prophecies of the paradise heavens are fulfilling in every nation of all things said and done. The different and undetermined times face the people daily clearing the way for eternal life on earth. The distinguished times and seasons of prophetic judgments clear the way to a new heavens on earth.

The judgments of God and God's people are at various times and periods in the universe

God's Equal Living Conditions

as we know it to be the work of God. It is the perfect peaceful will of God that reigns in outward forces of the air in the earth, clasped the clouds together makes the thunder roar in control of all people, places, and things. The authorship of this prophetic Prophet has been predicted to come is in accuracy already at hand. The history of the world's paradise earth is being called by the spirits of God and God's people. The messages of God are being described and revealed in the listening ears and visionary eyes of the greatest prophet that has ever walked the earth in your times and seasons. The terrible effects of God and God's people's judgment call are at hand as God saves many people from destruction. The development of new spiritual

God's Equal Living Conditions

waves is in the air with a powerful force of judgments and justice upon the people.

The people in the earth respond to the judgments of God and God's people. The call of judgment and justice brings much sorrow and grieves many people in the earth. The vision of a paradise earth is taking place in every life in future scenes of good and bad situations among the people. The judgments of God and God's people against unrighteousness every day are real. The unrighteous is charged with specific judgments of dishonesty, lies, injustice, malice, and secrets uncovered. The people in the earth face judgment daily as God favor many people saved unto eternal life. The new heaven on earth is forming from the powerful angels of God. The earth will be very different from the earth we know. The greedy are brought to shame by the powerful spirits of God and God's people in the earth. The spirits of God are using the powerful anointed angels of God. The unrighteous are defeated by the righteous people who inherit eternal life on a paradise earth.

The days are forming the way to a paradise earth as the people of God rejoice in heaven on earth. The spiritual angels of God and God's people are set free from the burdens of the world. The destructions of judgment destroy the peace of all unrighteousness. The spiritual minded people represent God and God's kingdom paradise heaven forming on earth. The final prophecies are now fulfilling heaven on earth.

God's Equal Living Conditions

The just judgments of God and God's people punish unrighteousness. The stiff necked - people are caught in the crossfire of judgment and justice every day. The historical order of judgment and justice set in the earth over power stubbornness in a terrible judgment call. The spirits of the people in the earth are sensitive to the spirits of God and God's people because there is nothing left undone leading to the paradise earth.

The suffering conditions of the people change by their praying spirits as their prayers are answered by the spirits of God. The people are guaranteed equal treatment on a paradise earth with heaven on earth. The end of stressful times surfaces as the outbreak of God and God's people's powerful spirits prevail. The victory of

God's Equal Living Conditions

God and God's people appears in control as all spirits in the earth unite as one and the same on one big Holy land. The latter day spirits of the people appear joyful to receive eternal life. The brighter days are ahead unto all who endure until the end of all sins in the earth.

8

The Latter Days Declared Daily

The latter days are declared daily in the earth as the spirit of God roams the earth in natural relationships of the Holy people walking the earth with spirits of God within. The Prophet spirits of the highest Prophet to ever walk the earth in your time is present in the earth speaking to the spirits of God. The spirits of truth about the

God's Equal Living Conditions

return of God in the earth are here representing eternal life. The spirits of the Highest, are unknown to the people, are the spirits of God given to the highest by the spirits of God spiritually roaming the earth. The spiritual messages from God in the earth watching the people. The people do not know that God has come in the mystery and ways not expected to the eyes of the people. The spirits of God are changing people with unfaithfulness and disbelief in the spirits of God. The people are living in false belief that the return of Jesus is before them. The people must cross over into the spirits of God and listen because they have been misled.

The people set before the realness of God are in a very confused state of mind because they

God's Equal Living Conditions

are looking for something that is not going to happen. The spirits of God save people who repent of their sins having forgiven sins among themselves. The living reality referenced by the spirits of God belongs to God. The spiritual law of God set before the confusions in the world of people knowing not the truth. The spiritual heart and mind are signs that God spirits have never left the earth. The same as saying God has never left the earth. The people have not followed true sound doctrine. The national corruption of the people is in judgment. The national angels of God are roaming the earth in search of injustice and calling judgment on unfairness. The angels of God are aware of the spirits of the people's confused state of mind. There are many people not conscious of the eternal spirits of God in the earth. The dead do not rise in the earth and are unconscious eternally to the spirits in the earth. The people in the earth are being warned about their confused state of mind. The conducted state of mind is in danger of losing out on eternal life. It is time to cross over from the confused state of mine into real spirits of God.

The latter days angels pull out all things rotten to society. There is no option for people who turn a deaf ear to the spiritual truth that there is no return of Jesus, but they must operate from the spirits of God within them. There is danger in not receiving eternal life on a paradise earth. The spirits of God are supernatural spirits in all the earth. The people having superstitious

God's Equal Living Conditions

spirits needing to repent within are judgments of God and God's people upon them daily. The people know the difference between evil spirits and righteous spirits. There will be no superstitious faith entering eternal life on a paradise earth. The false-hood of religion is attacked by eternal judgments of God and God's angel people in the earth.

The exalted spirits of God's angels are in all the earth. The untrue false people who use God's name in vain to make money are punished in all the earth. The forces of God and God's people cleaning the earth of sins and disbelief of God are true and good spirits within self. The wicked and unjust cease in the earth as pure hearts receive the wealth of the unjust. The

God's Equal Living Conditions

greedy cease in the earth as the needy receive justice in the earth. The nations collapse in the midst of their corruption at the commands of God and God's people judging the earth. The latter days disasters of judgments and justice are upon the people. The commands of God's spirits speak obedience to righteous spirits within urging the people to repent of their confused state of mind. The people's confused state of mind tells them Jesus is soon to return are lies within their spirits. It is time to be professional in spirits in truth with common sense. The professional people of God's messages are guardian angels of interpreters of God's spirits. The wicked forces of a tragic mind have consequences that result in losing eternal life on a paradise earth. It is not good to abandon

God's Equal Living Conditions

the spirits of God and go your own way, knowing these are latter days of judgments and justice of God and God's people. These are times that all disbelief in the spirits of God shows up in daily lives. The unrighteous hearts of the people are powerless without directions.

    The latter days of spiritual judgment and justice are here in the earth as times change on the people quickly in a blink of an eye. The latter days of judgments are going around in the world calling peace and justice in equal treatment leading to eternal life on a paradise earth. It is God and God's people in the midst of the people calling judgment on the evil thoughts and unrighteous behaviors of the people. The guilty people stand before the judgments and justice in the whirl wind as God and God's people dial judgment and justice on all unrighteousness. The judgments and justice of God and God's people are upon all untrue thoughts of the people who believe that Jesus will return. These things falsely written are the reason why the people who wrote it were judged to eternal death for misleading the people.

The people have an opportunity to return to God's spiritual blessings that dwell within them. There are many people lost by their own spirits of troubled mind and refuse to comprehend the spiritual blessings of God and God's people. There are many warnings of God's blessings and curses upon the people in the earth. The people are scared to believe there is no

God's Equal Living Conditions

return of Jesus. The good news is the paradise earth is already forming and many will be left behind because of their beliefs in the return of a Prophet named Jesus that is not coming back again. The people in the earth cannot retaliate against the spirits of God and God's people. The laws of God command the creation of the paradise earth. The justice of God and God's people takes revenge on unrighteousness. The land and the people in the earth belong to the spirits of God. It was the spirits of God that called the earth into existence in the beginning of time. There will be many spirits among the people in the earth daily before them.

There is now among the people a person, a woman's spirits restoring the people in the

God's Equal Living Conditions

earth to obedience in spirits in truth so that the people quickly pick up on and act on the spirits of God that dwell deep within them. The laws of the land change to the good of the people instead of against the people. The old land and land marks wear themselves out of existence. The fears of God's judgments are upon the people daily in all things said and done daily bringing obedience to the spirits of God within you. The chosen people of God send out special spirits operating in the earth. The spirits of order and peace roam the earth. It is obvious the judgment spirits of God's destruction are operating and witnessed in the earth taking its toll on the people. The forces of restoration of God and God's people are in the earth calling a thing as though it was and it appears.

The spirits of God said to the people, you see what they are doing as I have called you to see. The times are now times to obey my voice and walk in all the ways I command you. The many stubborn stiff necked people with evil hearts are walking backwards and not forward to an eternal paradise earth. I the Lord commanded the Highest Priest Prophet to speak to this people and tell them I said this is the voice of the Lord that speaks and not you of your own. There is no Jesus to come to them at no time now neither in the future. Their spiritual minds have been misled from times of the beginning of time came into existence from the disobedience of Adam and

God's Equal Living Conditions

Eve. The evil confused hearts are an abomination that closed their way to eternal living equal on a paradise earth said the Lord. The spirits of the Lord God speak to the people. It is not the spirit of Jesus; I, the Lord, your God, am God all by myself. I, the Lord, make a voice in the land be heard as I, the lord, your God, have called it to be. The Prophet of the highest has spread out before heaven on earth in spirits in truth that I, the Lord your God, brought upon you. The people before the Prophet hath backslid and are very confused given heed to repent. The law of the Lord is with the Highest Priest Prophet ever walked the earth in your times of now. The people are ashamed as I, the Lord, overthrow them; there is no wisdom in them.

God's Equal Living Conditions

I, the Lord your God, gather the people up and bring distress on them, and they feel it if they don't come to themselves and receive the truth about there is no return of Jesus. These things cause them not to prosper in wealth. The power of the Prophet of the highest is established stretching out in the heavens on earth calling it as it appears. The people are without knowledge under a false image. The people are under worthless delusions as the form their own perish nested upon themselves. The signs exist in the land as the Lord your God is already here paving the way for eternal life with heaven on earth. The signs of the latter day's visions are fulfilling on the people each day. The times are saying woe while the foolishness of the people in this world ceases.

God's Equal Living Conditions

The people that followed the path of the unrighteousness fall the same way into the dust of the earth. Many people do not see the way of God. There are those who look for self gain in every situation, but refuse to help others. There is no prejudice entering eternal life in heaven on earth forming daily in all the earth without fail.

9

The Judgment of God's People Prevail

The words of God sent through the Prophet are no-longer delayed but come quickly with life being so uncertain each second. I, the Lord, am real answered the Prophet I sent to you. I the Lord your God say to you the Prophet is real

God's Equal Living Conditions

that I sent to inform you that you have been deceived in thinking Jesus is returning to earth. The people in the days of the Bible being written did not believe in Jesus and did not believe the things I, the Lord, told Jesus to tell them just like the people are today. The days of my people prevail forming each day before disbelievers in confusion brought by the price of mankind to all who believe Jesus is returning to earth. These things are not so. I, the Lord, Your God speak to you in spirit in truth.

The people have failed to see the signs of judgment before their very eyes daily every second prevailing in the earth. I, the Lord, your God say to you the day will come when it will be against the law to carry a Bible, and you will know

God's Equal Living Conditions

a change has come. The changes that form do not need Bibles in the paradise earth of eternal peace. I live said the Lord your God as I bring my words written and spoken into manifestation through the spirits of my people. I, the Lord, your God say to you people, the signs of a higher spiritual return are before you in spirits in truth in the highest Priest Prophet in flesh and blood forming times and season of heaven on earth. The times are now times of value I, the Lord, your God bring you. The forgiven sinners believe there is no Jesus to come now neither to come in the future. The forgiven sinners believe I the Lord your God is God all by my-self.

The now times of God's judgments upon the people prevail instantly. The people are punished for believing in a false God of their own thoughts of Jesus return. There are many people who find it hard to believe the Highest Priest Prophet that has ever walked the earth in their times and seasons. I, the Lord, your God set my face against false worship of the people in confusion of Jesus' return not happening. I, the Lord your God, make these words known in all the earth: there is no Jesus to come now neither in the future. The presence of my spirits prevails in all the earth. I, the Lord your God, say to you my justice calls judgments. The ways of mine are just and real in the earth I, the Lord your God, say to you. I, the Lord, say to you my hooks are in every strong hold are laid waste and snares in every direction in the earth. The earth is stripped

God's Equal Living Conditions

of the wicked evil hearted in judgment and justice in the sight of all people in the earth. The wrath of eternal judgment is in the earth. The words of the Highest Priest Prophet manifest before the people's very eyes. The manifestation of God is as quick as lightening striking on earth. The things the Highest Prophet speak and write are upon the people in an instant.

There are no confusions in the paradise eternal earth about the return of Jesus. I, the Lord your God, have come to receive you in spirits and in truth as God all by myself. The forces of God and God's people make plain the ways of God in all the earth. The works of God prevail in all power quickly identified. The visions lights are flashing forming spiritual prophecies as God and

God's Equal Living Conditions

God's people spiritually roam the earth calling things needed in the paradise eternal earth. The radical change everyone sees taking place as struggling in the earth ceases. The people in the earth learn to trust God and God's people's power operating in the earth. The prevailing spirits in the earth operate year after year until sin ceases in the earth renewing spiritual minds. The perfect boldness of God and God's people's spirits has given the people eternal hope in God.

The spirits of God and God's people surround every part of the earth. The spirits of God renew natural laws until no natural laws are needed in the earth. The earth forms into one big Holy land. The people see the health of the people working to the good of the people in many different ways. The prevailing promises of God are in place in the earth. There are many warnings before the people to take heed and follow the spirits of God within them that have been ignored by sinful hearts cannot enter eternal life. The spirits of God and God's people convert the people and cover the whole earth. The restoring of the people and the earth converts the earth to heaven on earth restored back to its proper use and purpose from the beginning when God created heaven on earth.

The cleansing of the people's hearts and desecration of the earth clear the way to eternal living on a paradise earth. The various occasions of bad weather take place all over the earth. The things that govern the people that are not good for the benefit of the people wear it out as it ceases from among the people. The wipe out of many people, places, and things shows signs all over the earth when the harvest of independence of equal treatment is taking place. The people refuse to be misled by others blocking their way to eternal life on a paradise earth. The people trust the spirits of God heard within their hearts saying cross over to the newness of eternal life. The people are victorious as God answers their prayers forming the heavens on earth. The spirits of God released the change in the hearts of the people misled.

The betterment of the people forms in the earth as the people accept changes in their lives. The earth is being redesign to the forming of a

God's Equal Living Conditions

paradise earth during differences between other nations of people. The new world order is forming spiritually and physically as many events occur. The events lie in the spiritual power of God and God's people. The real significance of God and God's angels spirits prevails over all the earth. It is God and the angels of God uttering the judgment that's changing the earth and the people in the earth every second of every minute. The government of the people wears itself out in judgments and justice of God and God's people prevailing over the earth. The spell of judgment is being realized upon the people every-day in life. It is God and the angels of God speaking to the spirits of God into the air. The earth retains the spirits of new hope in the air over all the earth

God's Equal Living Conditions

that controls the spirits of the people in all the earth.

The times and seasons are now in the plain the Highest Priest Prophet ever in your times and seasons writing and speaking according to the spirits of God called to her hearing spirits. It is the angels of God that have taken charge according to the spirits of God in the earth. The new world orders of a paradise earth forms in the minds of the people making decisions that affect the people's daily lives. It is God's miraculous spiritual angels spiritual powers that enhance the minds of the people to the update of spirits according to the purpose of an appointed paradise earth called by the spirits of God and God's people. The people of God's minds are

God's Equal Living Conditions

entertained by various spirits of a paradise heaven on earth. The people are entertained by various spiritual angels unknowingly. The spiritual angels of God cover every ground of the earth. The move of God covers every individual in the earth constantly forming the new world order of peace and happiness.

The established explicit historical new world order happens rapidly as tough conditions rise all over the world. The chosen people are a special people of God called angels operating in the spiritual realm of God. It is time the people are aware that I the Lord your God, have come up from the spiritual heaven on earth to receive all believers of these words in this book written and spoken to you. I, the Lord your God, am in mid air

God's Equal Living Conditions

in the earth operating in the people of good spiritual minds who receive me. I, the Lord your God, say to you be not dismayed at what you read and hear in your spirits, but receive it to be true. I, the Lord your God, am before you calling judgments in all the air of the earth over all disbelief attitudes. It is time to go on forming the paradise earth and not staggering where you or people have been misled about the return of Jesus is not happening.

It is time to get over your feelings and move on with eternal life on a paradise earth. The whole wide world of people stands in the spirits of God and God's people. The spirits of God and God's people are persistently destroying sins governing humankind that provoke the wrath of judgment call. The furious spark of judgment does not have pity on anyone. The ignorance of the people misled about the return of Jesus is not happening is no excuse in every nation of people. The various religions have failed and misled the people. The doors of the Holy spirits are closed from foolish people who have refused the messages of God's spirits sent to them. The mysterious ways of God are being performed in all the earth.

There is no reason to be in search of which way to go as I the Lord your God bring these words written and spoken to you in this book. The people will continue to face ridiculed terrorism that are in disbelief of these words written and the people who are unjust. It is justice prevailed

God's Equal Living Conditions

all over the whole earth. The faith of the people safe guards them into eternal life. The vengeance of God's judgment attacks the unjust people. It is I the Lord your God having a natural concern for the people to inherit the paradise heavens on earth under peaceful conditions. I the Lord your spiritual God say to you have no doubt about eternal living, but receive it in all you say and do to inherit eternal life.

10

The People's Minds Controlled by Spirits Within

The people's minds are controlled and consol by spirits of God and God's people. The prophetic history of God and God's people's judgment call is in existence in the earth. The messages of God are fulfilling in this spiritual world we live in of good and bad spirits of the people. This book you read is from the call of God through the Biblical author of the Highest Priest Prophet ever walked the earth during your time in this spiritual world. The set period of the renewal of the earth and the people in the earth is here. The spiritual forces of God and God's people are at work forcefully by spirits of God. These are the appointed times of God answering the people's prayers in a more fixed instant way according to the need in the paradise earth forming. The spiritual forces of God and God's people recognize that the angels of God are very successful in the earth.

The people are in an outrage over the historical unjust treatment and unfairness forced

God's Equal Living Conditions

upon the unfortunate people. The unfair treatments of others govern the people in every aspect of life. The unfair treatments of the people fading out do not enter the paradise earth. The evil days of the unjust fade out to the ways of every unjust person's ways are in punishment of God and God's people's judgments and justice. The wrath of God and God's people's judgments is already upon the people without notice and without fail no-one escape the latter day judgments and justice upon the people whether good or bad judgment. It is God in the background of the spiritual angels roaming the earth judging all things said and done in the earth in every part of the earth.

God's Equal Living Conditions

The people of God call things as though they were, and God answers them. The complete massacre of renewing the earth is to save the people of God and complete the paradise earth disposing the end of sin. The journey of renewing the earth and the people's spirits in the earth is a long process which already has been formed. The people have confidence and trust in the spirits of God. The unjust have been insubordinate to the ways and spirits of God and God's people. The insubordination of the people to the spirits of God cease in every part of the earth. The unfair practice of forbidden racial prejudice practice governing the people with unfairness in judgment. The people are bitter and stressed out with deep grief for loved ones who have passed

God's Equal Living Conditions

on never to return to the earth. The prayers of the people have prompted God and God's people to take action despite the times and seasons of the years before them.

The times and seasons of unhappy people are in full gear in all the earth. The things going on in the earth daily are at a constant change. It is God and God's people watching everything as the people give an account of their individual lives daily to the judgments of God. The present concerns are for a just and faithful world treating everyone equally forming the paradise earth. The earth and the people in the earth are being repaired and fixed according to eternal living. The opportunity for eternal living starts right now with you living a righteous heart. These are times and seasons your faith and patience give an account of your actions within things said and done each day.

The people become one nation under God with justice for all in one big Holy land redeemed from unjust treatment. The people are committed to obedience to God in a paradise earth with their own trust and independence on themselves. The people are over their own lives entering the paradise earth abiding by the laws of God for eternal living. The people abide by every spirit of God that abides within them having authority over themselves. This is a reminder that the eyes of God's spirits are the people of God's spirits all over the earth. The people are in contact with God's angels in the world are God's

God's Equal Living Conditions

people in the world unknown to the eyes of many people. The angels of God walk around in the earth dispensing their spirits all over the earth. The angels of God call rebellious spirits into judgment and the justice of God controlling the spirits of the people. The unjust spirits are not under cover as the people of God know the thoughts of the unjust in every part of the earth. The good and bad deeds of the people are taken into account as they stand before judgment of God daily.

The sign of the Prophet's presence in the earth is present in spirits in truth as the prophet hears and sees all things forming in the paradise earth. The Prophet sees and hears the spiritual words of God calling all things to cease that is not needed in the paradise earth. The many eye sights of God's people are seeing and hearing all over the earth in every part of the earth. The real Prophets of God are real people in the earth sent by God spiritually to redeem the people back to God entering eternal living. The people having God's spiritual existence are in all the earth with all the constant promises of God. The renewing of the earth has been called into existence by the Highest Priest Prophet ever to walk the earth in your time. The renewing of the earth has already risen up in every part of the earth. The spirits of God are in the people of God eternally and will never cease from the earth.

    The spirits of God are effective in every way. The spirits of the people are committed to

God's Equal Living Conditions

God in every way. The Prophet of the Highest has divine spiritual authority in the earth. The undistinguishing spirits of God and God's people roam over all the earth. The people are privileged to be in the presence of God and God's people's spirits in the earth. Many people from many different life styles, who are viewing these messages of God in agreement, have been waiting to hear the good news of the paradise eternal life style. There will be no-one redeemed from the laws of God's eternal living. The pit-falls of life are uncertain, but eternal life is not uncertain. The instant orders of God have already been called in all the earth. The Prophet of this book is telling you exactly what God is saying to the people who have a need to enter eternal

God's Equal Living Conditions

living. The Prophet of God is in clear fellowship with the spirits of God's power. The people of God are in clear fellowship with God. The reality of God is clearly brought to mind in full maturity of the mind with common sense measuring all things you read in this book. The predictions of this Prophet which have been studied and talked about, is now here.

The kingdom of God is at hand forming eternal life. The sure facts of the future of the people are at hand. The repentance of the people is at hand. The people have needs to come to themselves in common sense. God is the end result of all things said and done in the earth. In every situation righteous standards dominate the earth in spirits in truth. The radiance of God in

God's Equal Living Conditions

person is in the Prophet fore-told about these times to come which are now here. The powerful Prophet occupies God's throne in spirits, in truth, and in predictions in the earth. The wickedness of all the earth is exposed in every part of the earth. The judgments and justice of God and God's people pierce through darkness unseen in the earth leading to eternal living. The spirits of God and God's people dictate any unrighteousness anywhere in the earth. The pressure of God and God's people is felt in every part of the earth.

The spirits of God and God's people destroy every sin committed in the earth and pave ways to eternal living on the paradise earth. The Highest Priest Prophet's books are books of prophecies and visions appearing in the earth, are

God's Equal Living Conditions

a complete reply from spirits of God and God's people. The people see the presence of God and God's people move things in the earth without notice to the people in many situations. The presence of God and God's people follow the dark clouds in every part of the earth. The everyday judgments of God and God's people are pronounced against the unrighteousness every day. The visions of God's people are spread in every whirlwind in the earth. The spiritual forces of all the angels of God are in every world-wind in the earth. The unrighteous do not go unpunished by the judgment powers in every world-wind. The rich of the unrighteous ones no-longer build off of the poor. The judgments of God are upon every malpractice forced on the people seen and unseen. The world falls into place slowly, but surely. The people escape unfair rules and regulations in society.

The blow-out of sin in the earth is at hand as a clean sweep takes place in every part of the earth. The many changes in the earth taken place continue to change until the paradise earth is complete as many things change.

The people face more chronological historical true events from reliable visions of the real truth of the people of God. The people of God are linked to true spirits of God. The results of judgments and justice in the earth are a clear call of how it is finished from the highest person of God. The modern events are different from events of before ever on the face of the earth.

God's Equal Living Conditions

The act of God is in every part of the earth as the unrighteous answer to the judgments and justice of God. The actions of God and God's words prevail in all the earth. The actions of God now exist in the world like never before in many mysteries. The actions of God are threshing and spreading all over the world in an instant. The sudden happening of many things are happening all over the world. The sign of things to come are already in the earth. The plans of God for the people are in the earth as the plans of the unrighteous wears itself out of the earth in the judgments of God. The slaughter of the unrighteous upon the people ceases.

11

The Slaughter of Famine Destroyed

The seasons and times of the unrighteous are scattered and cease in every land by the powerful centralized spirits of God and God's people. The destruction of the unrighteous is violent gives and account in judgment and justice.

God's Equal Living Conditions

The unrighteous are driven out of existence. The people are charged in judgment with their royal unrighteousness. The people of unrighteousness are under the spirits of the angels of God after God's own heart. The glory of the presence of God has entered every space in the earth and is the angels of God as the angels utter eternal living. The approval of God's judgments is in every part of the earth called according to deeds done. God has given instruction to the angels according to the need of judgment called in the earth. The judgments upon the people in the earth belong to God and the Holy one given to the people of God to judge the people according.

The days and years are chronologically unraveling judgments and justice daily is real showing effect in every part of the world. There are times when things happening in one end of the earth from time to time happen all over the earth. The wickedness of money is destroyed all over the world. The monetary ties to power of unrighteous cease in judgment and justice. The consequences of dishonesty and disloyalty are weakening and cease in judgment the drive of the people over powering the people in poverty. The national effects of God's invasions of judgments and justice are felt and recognized all over the world. There be many cities and countries abandoned in the call of God's judgments upon the people. The call of judgment is upon poverty and rich alike in search of righteous hearts. In the universe of the world God's power uncovers all

God's Equal Living Conditions

the hidden wealth in the world. The people give reference to the power of God.

There is no doubt in the minds of the people referencing the judgments and justice call of God and God's people's power operating in the earth. The people are being judged with supreme justice and judgments. The conduct of the unrighteous is judged daily by the effects geared wrongfully toward the people. It is God above every cry whether cry for joy or cry for help. The answer to many prayers are now being answered by God as many prayers are answered according to the will of God. It is God spreading the clouds in a roar of thunder in anger with the people's unrighteousness. It is God breaking the people with judgments and justice all over the world. It is

God's Equal Living Conditions

God putting the imagination of the people into reality from the false thoughts they serve. It is God confronting the unjust in all things said and done in the earth in judgment. It is the majesty of God creating a new world with eternal order. In the new world order every unrighteous person is powerless. The justice of God is dangerous to sin consistently.

The people realize God speaks to a clear conscience reversing the unconscious mind to a spiritual mind set. The feelings of particular circumstances are stirred up by the emotions of God and God's people. The problems of life are the cry-out of the people treated unfairly saying justice needs to be served on unrighteous. Notice of judgment has now been served on the

God's Equal Living Conditions

unrighteous operating daily bringing world order to a paradise earth. The individual difficulties of life's poverty turn into blessings of God eternally, living on a paradise earth. It is all things in life changing where change is needed in seasons and time. It is the ultimate answer of God's promise to the people. The people become aware of certain future signs of the Messiah God judging the people in every part of the earth. It is all things judged said and done big or small, poor or rich, and good or bad.

The quick divine judgment of the people going on every-where in the world has struck the earth already. There are many people who did not know that the judgments and justice of God have struck the earth. There are blessings in

God's Equal Living Conditions

reading these spiritual messages and visions from God to the people in every part of the world. It is good to set your hearts and mind on the judgments of God preparing a paradise earth forming to the good of the people. The future of the wicked cease's along with a world of conspiracy people. The spirits of God and God's people depict sins of unrighteousness before it happens. The total judgments of God delegate spiritual power and spiritual authority. God has sent the angels of God to deliver the people out of poverty of the hand of the unrighteous in every part of the earth. The scriptures are now brought under the promises of God. This means one must receive God's spirits through belief and faith in order to be blessed with the promises of God.

God's Equal Living Conditions

I, the Lord your God, examine your faith, hearing, and spirits. I, the Lord your God, have sent you a sign of the covenant promise. The spiritual guidance within Holiness leadership brings spiritual order and purposes of God's eternal living. The faith of the people of God reveals spiritual order of restoring the people to spiritual minds. The people of God inherit the paradise earth. The people receive the angels of God's instructions for eternal living. God promises to give understanding to the people referencing the new world order. The people of God give the people signs of God's promises operating in the earth in their presence. The slaughter of famine ceases from among the people in every part of

God's Equal Living Conditions

the earth. The presence of God is with the people of God's spiritual being in every part of the world.

The promise of God's return to the earth is here within the presence of the people of God's spirits. The Holy people of God who are heavenly sent are the results of the promises of God who come to receive the people through the Holy people of the land. The people of God have free spirits to warn the people God is present within their open clean spirits. The people are God's grace and hopes working through faith in God help the people in the world to understand how to receive fellowship with God. The circumstances do not change God is a spirit. The spirits of God are felt and heard from within self. The trust of self is the main key to trust what you hear God

God's Equal Living Conditions

say to your spirits within you. The people of God persuade the people to have confidence in self with free course and free will to trust their own spirits to inherit eternal life. The spirits of the Holy people are God's spirits in God. The spirits of the Holy Priest are not subject to the laws of God, but must abide by the spirits of God within as God gives directions to lead the people to eternal living.

The spirits of God are subject to the Prophets as having the last say so in words from God with decent order in the Holy Temples of God. The Holy Priests are Elders, Bishops, Prophets, and Evangelists. The spirits of the Holy people have direct contact with God's spirits of God's desires for the people's eternal living. The spirits of the Holy people are controlling spirits that lead the people to eternal life. The Holy people of God have spirits to give and take where needed leading to eternal life. The Holy people of God have spiritual eyes to see near and far. The Holy people of God have spiritual ears to hear near and far. The Holy people of God obey the spirits of God and judge the earth near and far. The famines of the earth have no place on the paradise earth forming daily.

The people give thanks to God for many treasures leading to eternal living on a paradise earth in every part of the world. The cease of famine in the earth never returns to earth again. The people in the world get joy from gathering the harvest of eternal living. The reaping of what

God's Equal Living Conditions

God has planted for the people is now here. The natural desires of the heart of the people have changed to eternal desires of the heart. The spirits of the people are for eternal living on a paradise earth free of sin, sickness, and death. The people do not get tired of standing strong until the end of all sins in the earth cease. The people learn to obey the spirits within them, a physical force of God leading to eternal living. The people standing strong do not let the famines of life trouble them by letter nor by speech knowing God is in control with the last say so to every situation happening in life among the people.

    The people experiencing the Bible scriptures come forth before their eyes and ears the realness of God and God's Holy people. The

God's Equal Living Conditions

forming of eternal living is announced through-out the world. This thing spoken to the people depends on their strict obeying of the spirits of God. It is time to realize the realness of God operating in your life. It is time to know everything is going to be alright. Those who do not obey the spirits of God within are in failure of entering eternal life when all sickness, sin, and death have ceased from the earth. The people must recognize and obey every spirit of God within them. The people must live spiritual faith through-out the famines of life obeying spirits of God within self. The people must recognize eternal life depends on your own well-being and faith. It is time for the people to take care of their self and care about living eternally. There are

God's Equal Living Conditions

many people living now who will not make it to eternal living. The famines of this world cease at the commands of God and God's Holy people.

12

Spirits of God and God's People Remain Forever

There will not be anyone who will rise from the grave as it is known death is eternal death. It is time for the people to do all that is required of them by the spirits of God. It is clearly seen and heard the times are now times for the

God's Equal Living Conditions

people to live faithfully making all things right with the spirits of God and treating all people equally. The plan of God is to bring a heavenly paradise world into existence daily forming. The people every-where in the earth have need to live out God's plan receiving eternal life on a paradise heaven on earth. It is time for the people to live in unity with one another in oneness with God. The people speak God's Holy spirits into existence of a paradise world become real in life. There will be nothing hidden from the spirits of the Holy people. The things done in the dark are seen and heard in the spirits of the Holy Priests. The people of God have a large measure of wisdom and insight with every spiritual being and spiritual blessings in the world.

God's Equal Living Conditions

The times are now times of bringing everything into existence according to the will of God for the people on a paradise earth. The spirits of God reveal things to the Holy people of God. The spirits of God and the Holy people are forever and will never cease. It is God who brings light to what the spiritual mind sees and hears. The promise of great blessings from God are forming daily in the world. The people of God have great spiritual power and strength from on high leading them to eternal living. The troubles of this world are under the feet of the people because God is the ruler of authority, has taken place. The Holy people in leadership were called at birth for such times as these according to the

God's Equal Living Conditions

spirits of God to lead the people to eternal life. There are no failures in the spirits of God.

The spirits of God living in the people of God are known to the people. The spirits of the Holy Prophets and Holy Priest are from God's authority with approval. The Holy people are special gifts from God. The special powerful inner spirits of each individual help them to be strong and endure until the end. The Holy people of God with God's power stand broad, long, high, and deep. The nature of God's spirits is in the Holy people of God. The Holy people of God have measured up to the standards of God in spirits and in truth. The Holy people of God are bound together in spiritual peace. The appointed times such as now times are times God wants the

God's Equal Living Conditions

people to come together in the Holy temples and become as one big Holy land. The times are now times to be strong in spite of troubles, sickness, sins, and death. The people in the world must endure until all things that are not eternal cease in the earth.

The people must take control of their lives and style of life. The things of God are revealed to the holy people of God and are spoken boldly to the people. The holy church leaders in leadership have deep effect on the people. The light of the holy people of God comes from God in the likeness of God. These messages written and spoken reach the servants of God. The lights of God's people shine in darkness for the sake of the people from God. The knowledge of God shines in

God's Equal Living Conditions

the face of all of God's Holy people forever. The spiritual treasures of the Holy people are supreme power from God. The holy people of God trouble the people. It is life eternal at work in the lives of the people in the world. The spirits of God speak to the faith of the people. It has been the spirits of God that have raised the world up to this very time and hour. The Holy people of God reach many people by their presence in many situations in the Temple and out of the Temple.

The physical being of the people is renewed daily and must endure until the end of a temporary life style. The sufferings of the people have brought them eternal glory from God. There are many things seen as not eternal, and the things unseen are forming eternal living. It is the

God's Equal Living Conditions

Lord your God has clothed you and transformed you into eternal life with a guaranteed spirit full of faith and courage. It is time to receive what you deserve according to the will of God. The people of God are the character of God that is recognized by many people. The renewed being of each individual is eternal spirits and eternal body for people who make it until the end of all sins are over.

These messages written to you are from the spirits of God and God alone. The spirits of God changing people that are within the union of connecting with their inner spirits is God speaking to you. It is the spirits of God in you connected with all ideas you have in mind for eternal living. The times are now times that God is ready to show the people favor. The people must patiently endure the last and evil days of the people. These troubles and difficulties of life end in judgments and justice of God and God's people judging the people of unrighteousness. The spirits of God honor and defend the righteous hearted people. It is good to stay away from unclean people mentally and physically. The times are now times to stay purified in spirits and truth. It is time to stay encouraged knowing God is renewing the people that endure until the end of all sins, sickness, and death.

The people of God are specially made in the image of God mentally and physically. The people of God act on what God requires of them in the physical being. The people of God stir up their spiritual gifts working in the physical being. The people of God are highly respected. It is the spirits of God that stir up the people of God's gift according to need in and out of seasons. The people of God perform their gifts bringing glory to God. The deep grace of God is in the people of God. The forces of God rule the people of God and everyone in the earth according to eternal life forming. The forces of God powerfully raise knowledge to the standards of eternal living. The outward appearance of the people of God is the appearance of God in spirits in physical body. The spirits of God renew the appearance of the people of God. The mental being of the people of God shows their authority with God with strong words and encouragement to the people. The

God's Equal Living Conditions

people of God that are appointed to judge the people have high standards beyond limits to measure the people by.

The Holy Leaders of God are judging the people without respect of person. These things mentioned in this book are already set with the forces of God in the earth over the entire world already. The work of the people of God is not limited but already set before the people of God. The people of God' new being is the appearance of God character. The people of Holy leadership are the appearance of God's image and character. The Holy people of God do not allow anyone in their circle that is not worthy of eternal life. The people of God have favor with God and are not influenced by others. The people of God live

God's Equal Living Conditions

completely Holy and apart from the people unholy. The people of God have courage and joy referencing the things of God and eternal life forming.

The troubles of the world and quarrels are everywhere in the world. The people in the world change their ways of doing things and cross over to eternal living forming. The word is you must be careful with people that cause you sadness, hardship and may harm you robbing you of eternal living. The word is to be without fault of discomfort as I the Lord your God make these things plain to you written. The people have a need to cheer up from disappointments as you grow stronger in faith in God and God's people. The works of God depend on the people of God

God's Equal Living Conditions

strongly and faithfully. The people in Holy leadership have free course of free will with the spirits of God. The will of God is accomplished in the people of God in leadership and in any capacity of leadership in the world. The people in Holy leadership have a special knowledge, faith, speech, and services to lead the people to eternal life. The Holy people of God are rich in all things they have need of. The will of God is not based on wants, but is based on eternal living on a paradise world living out of the special purpose and plans God stared from the beginning of time.

The will of God works with the need for a paradise heavens on earth over the whole world. There are many people in need of good quality treatment from other people surrounding them.

God's Equal Living Conditions

The people are judged instantly on fair treatment of others. This is the will of God and the people of God. The Holy people of God are appointed for God's glory and high praise and purpose of eternal living. The days of the unjust are numbered accordingly. The people of the world are in the judgment sight of God and God's people daily. The people of God are a sign sent by God operating in the earth.

The names Holiness alone stir up the people's thoughts as the people of God represent a Holy God. The people of God destroy strong holds by pulling down obstacles and advance the people to higher heights in different levels of eternal living. The people of God are loyal and obey the voice of God at all times. The outward

God's Equal Living Conditions

seen appearance of the people of God shows that their character which is built from the holy spirits of God. The forces of God force the people of God to judge the people instantly. The forces of God guard the people of God.

13

Difficult Times Removed from the Heaven which is on the Earth

The people have caused difficulties times by their own standard ways of living for monetary purposes to measure themselves by which are limited standards. The standards of God are beyond the limits of the people's mind. The

God's Equal Living Conditions

eternal things forming in the world works to the good of the people of God. The people in world are limited by the people in the earth. It is clear the spirit of God is complete in the people of God. The spirits of God take charge of all things ordered to be in eternal living. The promises of God are in the light of the earth. It is the Lord your God at the gates of eternal living. The people in the world are limited by difficult times. I, the Lord your God, speak through an open spiritual heart within your life. The visions and revelations happen from the words spoken from the spirits of God. The things written in this book, seen, and heard come true are true. These words proved among the people and show God is among the people in the world.

God's Equal Living Conditions

It is the spirits of God which visit the people in difficult times with spiritual order leading to eternal living. The present order of God speaks to the people's spirits in everything they do and say in this world. The spirits of God visit the people by evidence to eye witness. The powers of God live and reign in the people of God in the world. The Holy people have proof God lives and speaks through them in the earth. The Holy people are the living truth of faith in God. The good news among the people is true facts about God's wonder working power seen and unseen. The people of God know the people who have faith in God. The spirits of God are saying the people of God are no longer misled by untruthful worthy people. The results of faith in

God have showed up in personal lives. The times like these are called by God accordingly. There will be no one to change the Holy gospel of God at no time.

The people are condemned to Hell that are not in agreement with Holiness. The people who condemn Holiness want to be popular with each other's approval because the Holy people of God are popular with each other's approval in God. It is I, the Lord your God who reveals these things the people in the world have a need to know. The churches of God in Christ practice true Holy religion in the sight of God and are a chosen people. The traditional churches in religion have ancestors who have tried to change the Holy ways of God. The money changers who are a den of

God's Equal Living Conditions

thieves using God's name for the purpose of self gain will cease in judgment call. The good news is the grace of God is for the people of God with true Holy faith in God. The people before the spirits of God are before the faces of God in spirits in truth and obtain information from God reference eternal living.

I God say to you these things written of me are in spirits in the air in my people and are true. There will be no one to persecute the written words of God unto you in judgments and justice. The faith of the people in the world is raised revealing the way to gospel eternal living. The Holy gospel of God is true and safe. The people that are contrary to the Holy gospel of God are condemned in judgment. I, the Lord your

God's Equal Living Conditions

God, am a powerful just God forming eternal living in judgments and justice. The Holy leaders in leadership recognize the tasks of God before them. The people clearly walk a straight and narrow path to eternal living enduring until the end of all unrighteous things. The people of God are righteous building toward eternal living. The spirits of miracles are before the people n the world forming eternal living. The times are now times of endurance relating to receiving eternal life. It is time to speak the word of God with courage. The people have a need to be truthful showing honor to God forming eternal living. The spirits of God are with the people in the world always.

God's Equal Living Conditions

A strong spiritual life brings good health to eternal living. The cost to receive eternal living is a high cost of a truthful and a Holy heart. The cost of discipleship is to be faithful and successful in life leading to eternal living. The written messages of God in this book mold the minds of the people in need of eternal living. The relationship of God's people flows in the world into the minds of the people. The believer's life style is different from those who do not believe God is spirits operating in the earth. The great crowds of people follow the Holy people of God. The prediction of the Holy people is popular. The Holy people of God are totally involved with the Holy spirits of God. The good news of God's actions and authority is in the world making lead way to eternal living.

God's Equal Living Conditions

The authority of powerful spirits is seen in the power of the people of God. The people of God are straight forward with the words of God.

The resurrection of judgment and justice in the earth has risen all over the world. The messengers of God have risen all over the world opening path ways to eternal living. The people are baptizing with Holy hands in Holy water. The Holy people of God cast their nets out and catch the people off guard reeling them into eternal life. The Holy people of God have authority over the spirits and make them obey at their command. The Holy people of God order spirits to obey the spiritual authority leading to eternal life. The news of the Highest Priest Prophet spread quickly over the world. The difficult times remove

God's Equal Living Conditions

and equal treatment for all people in the world from people in leadership. The hope for eternal living has risen destroying difficult times in the world. The latter days of difficult times are in judgments relating to equal treatment. The suffering ways forced upon the people cease in justice and judgment roaming the earth daily.

The signs of the Holy people of God and the highest Priest Prophet in the earth are here in the physical realm. The Holy people of God are a supreme symbol for God's hope. There are many people terrified and watching all things said and done in the world. The people's faith shows them that God is watching all things said and done in the earth and that is a judgment call. It is the now times God is watching from a distance through the people of God everywhere in the world. The thunders of God roll across the entrance of many people keeping them from entering eternal living. The people of the world are aware of the Holy angels of God all over the world. The people talk referencing eternal living forming in the world. The heavens are forming on earth leading to eternal life. The people all over the world hear about the Holy people of God. The whole armor of God is the strength of the people. The heavenly authority spoken by the people of God is words of God now put to actions.

The written words of this book encourage all Christian people ready to receive the truth about Jesus and God. The times are now times for spiritual immatureness to cease and experience

God's Equal Living Conditions

the truth about God and Jesus. The return of Jesus is not happening at no time now neither any time to come. There are many people already spiritually mature. The power of God stands firm in the Holy people of God. It is clearly God before the people of God. The people ask God for all things they have need of. It is God beyond humankind understanding. The people of God's do not worry about anything. The people of God's mind are filled with praise to God. The people of God have strength to face all things. The greetings of God sent to the people saying endure until the paradise earth appears. It is God with the people by way of the Holy spirits in the world.

The people in the world submit their lives to God to live Holy leading to eternal living. The

God's Equal Living Conditions

people of God have gospel spirits of love for the people. It is God fills the people of God with gospel eternal knowledge. The people have a need to endure with patience, contentment, and happiness is reference to eternal living. The Holy people of God have been reserved for times as these of today within the call of God. The Holy people are the kingdom light of God in every part of the world. The Holy people of God forgive the people of their sins that are sin that can be forgiven. The whole universe is under the strict supreme spiritual power of God and God's people. The proper things of God leading to eternal life are raised in the spirits of the people in order. The head of the Holy Temples is the spiritual authority of God. The Holy people of God are a sure foundation for the people to receive eternal life. The Holy people of God are the complete body of the church.

The Holy people of God perform the Holy secrets of God that are hid from mankind. The people of God bring the union of the people in order of spiritual maturity in the people entering eternal life. .The divine spiritual nature of God is in eternal living forming in all the earth. The Highest Priest Prophet is supreme over the people and rule spiritual authority. The lives of the people are favorable with God whose sins are forgiven sins as the people of God with spiritual authority leads the people to victory of eternal life. There are different ways of doing things that lead the people to eternal living. There is no

God's Equal Living Conditions

eating at the Holy Temples of God. The Holy Temples are for saving souls and burying the dead. The Holy people of God do not stray away from eternal guidance written and spoken by the spirits of the Holiest, Highest Supreme Being of the Holy Temples.

God's Equal Living Conditions

14

Declaring the Truth about God

The people are set free from unrighteous ruling spirits as they declare the truth about God and there is no return of Jesus. The people have been misled, now declares the truth. The spirits of the world are now under the submission of obeying the spirits of God and God's people. The people of God are called into one spiritual body of

God's Equal Living Conditions

wisdom leading to eternal life. The people do not become discouraged in all things said and done. The Holy people of God cleanse spirits near and far in all the earth. The Holy people of God teach and instruct, but in all things said and done give thanks to the Holy spirits of God. The people of God obey the spirits of God within self and are pleasing to God. It is the spirits of God that have given reference and approval to the spirits of the people of God. It is I, the Lord your God, speaking to you and making things clear to you. I, the Lord your God, say to you, "be fair and just in all things said and done in the earth." It is I, the Lord your God, saying to you; "be alert, be persistent in equal treatment of others."

God's Equal Living Conditions

It is I, the Lord your God, saying to you "lean not to your own understanding that is not equal with the spirits of the Supreme Being. It is time to be wise in your thinking and doing actions toward others. It is time to make pleasant speech always with an answer or with being silent with no answer." The news about the Supreme Being is traveling all over the world. The ways of God are too high for the people to figure out. The Holy people of God stand firm and convince eternal living is forming all over the world. The people of God personally hear from God within self. The Holy people of God do not forget the chain of leadership within the body of the Holy Temples. It is I, the Lord your God, with the people and I will

God's Equal Living Conditions

never leave you along. The times are now times to experience the truth about God.

The capital city of Florida establishes and experiences the risen spiritual works of God and God's people. The people of God stand firm in their decision making. The people of God are a chosen people with powerful words and powerful spirits of convictions geared toward the people entering eternal life. The spirits of the people of God imitate the spirits of God. The people are talking about the Highest Supreme Being are true spirits of God dwelling in the earth speaking and writing the good news in reference to eternal living. The word is God is operating in the world without notice to the people. The people of God cannot be tempted by any one. The truth is God is alive in the world in spirits in truth. The voice of God has come down from the spiritual heavens dwelling on earth. The spirits of God are in the air forming eternal living; be encouraged by these words. The people who reject the people of God reject not the people but reject God.

The people in this world must live a quiet and peaceful life and mind your own spirits that are before you. It is now you know the truth about eternal life and eternal death. There are those who have no hope for eternal life. It is I, the Lord your God, who is alive today in the earth as always and has never left the earth in spirits in truth. The believers of these words rise to higher heights in spirits. The people asleep in the spirits of God are not caught up with the people of God in spirits in truth. This is your time to receive the truth about God and be caught up in the Holy spirits of God with Holy believers of these words written. The things of God forms instantly in the world like a thief in the night. The people have relief declaring the truth about God. These words written are faithful and true prophecies. The Holy people of God are commanded by God not to become tired of judging the people, but continue in judgment until the end of all sins.

The people of God have a personal appeal that shows God's spirits are with them. The people of God are crowned with wisdom and knowledge from on high tearing down strongholds. The authority of God builds the people of God up. The Holy people of God stay within certain limits of people and things God put before them. The people of God are pure spiritual and Holy gospel complete. The Holy people of God are completely different from the people in world of lustful hearts. The people of God are a special people. The people of God have a disguised look of an angel with lights of righteousness. The Holy people of God perform many miracles proving God is real in their life. The Holy people of God are very intelligent with much educational experience. It is I, the Lord your God, love my Holy people calling all people to be Holy and righteous. The Holy people of God speak in the presence of God at all times. The peace of God rests, rules, and abides by the Holy people of

God's Equal Living Conditions

God. The people are no longer misled by false teaching.

It is I, the Lord your God, speak through the Holy people of God. The holy people of God keep a strict union with the spirits of God. There is plenty good room for all of God's people in the Holy Temples (kingdom) of God. The Holy people of God have the whole world in their hands calling the trumpets of God. The people in the world receive things by time and seasons. The Holy people of God have strict ruling spirits. These are the now times God gives the people all they have need of in the will of God forming eternal living. The Holy people of God pay attention to certain times, seasons, minutes, hours, days, months, and years. The Holy people

God's Equal Living Conditions

of God are angels of God very mature in spirits in truth. The Holy people of God tell people the truth about themselves. The Holy Priest Prophets in leadership do not prophesy to Holy leaders in leadership.

The Holy people of God have different attitudes and different spirits that come together as one and the same. The Holy people of God are spiritually formed by the spirits of God. It is I, the Lord your God, with spirits and truth now instantly before you. The Holy people of God speak among the people without argument defending their authority with God over the people. The spirits of God flow from the Holy people of God. The spirits of the people are natural results of their faith in God forming

God's Equal Living Conditions

eternal living. The spiritual minded people are spiritual beings images of God. It is I the Lord your God, saying Holy greetings to the Holy people of God having much work to do. This present time has been set in order for the Holy people of God to speak the gospel truth. The Holy Temples of Cogic has been stamped approved by the Holy spirits of God to judge, lead and guide the people to eternal living. The COGIC people are the chosen appointed people of God in righteous perfect standing with the spirits of God is God.

The Holy people see and hear what is true by way of the spirits of God. The forces of God are all over the COGIC leaders in leadership to judge the people of the world. The old things of this world are passing away as the new things of God

God's Equal Living Conditions

are forming eternal living everywhere. The changing times show that COGIC Holy people have favor with God to judge the people. There are many people judged silently and verbally. The times and seasons the people have been looking for are now here in their eye sight. It is time to crossover to the other-side and lean not to your own understanding. The days are days of true spirits and visions. The Holy people of God recognize Holy and truthful spirits within the people. There is nothing hid from the Supreme Being as all things are seen and heard in spirits and truth. The Holy people of God see and hear everything about the people before them near and far.

God's Equal Living Conditions

The works of God are alive in actions in spirits in the world forming eternal living. The facts about eternal living have been written to you declaring the truth about God. The Holy people of God have light in a dark place as there is nothing under the sun hid from them. The Holy people of God are the results that God's promises have come true in the earth. The fulfilling of the promise of God is present in the earth. The people who have been misled for decades must cross-over to the truth to make it into eternal life. There is no return of Jesus to come at no time in the world. The directions and guidance in this book are for the people who have needed to know how to enter eternal living on a paradise earth forming. The things of God forming are unknown to the eyes of the people. It is the now times and seasons for all people in this world to receive the truth about no return of Jesus and come to their-self within common sense.

The people now have light in darkness; they have lived in from their fore-fathers, teachings that are not true. Those that do not cross over in their beliefs will not receive eternal life on a paradise earth but have rejected eternal life. It is time to let the new spirits of God mold your mind into the new things of God forming in the world. The minds of the people have been blocked from the truth for such times as these that have been appointed for judgment upon every soul waiting for the return of Jesus. It is time to take away Jesus in your heart and go back

God's Equal Living Conditions

to God. It is time to insert God back into your heart without fail. I say to you go back to God in Holy spirits in truth in that you receive eternal life forming in a paradise heaven over the whole world. It is time to know you as a people do not have much time left to cross over to the truth as destruction in the world every day plays apart in the judgment call of God upon the people in the world. These words written are for believers of these words. The unbelievers are unevenly yoked and blocked from eternal life. The real truth of God set you free from all seen and unseen actions of unrighteousness before you daily. It is time for all people to come together as one and not be unevenly yoked by false teaching about the words of God. It is time to put common sense with these

God's Equal Living Conditions

words you read in this book and receive the truth. The times are now times to go back to God and put the misled spirits about Jesus behind you. The call of judgment is everyday upon all people living in this world. The choice is yours to reject or receive the good news in reference to the new things of God written to benefit you. The times are now time to search your soul and change your old thoughts to new thoughts before you in spirits in truth. There is no more miscalculations reference to the new world order. The times and seasons for new world order are here. The people's minds are asleep as they walk the earth and they stumble falling unaware of the newness of God as they look for the return of Jesus. The return of Jesus in their thoughts is not happening at any time.

It is time to walk with God and know that it is the works of God that destroy the works of the unrighteous ones. The people must use their time wisely believing the return of the paradise earth is forming. The people must realize the spirits of God is the higher power standing over the whole world. The promise of a paradise earth is here to change the lives of the people as they read these words from God to the people. The inconsistency on the part of many pastors has caused the people to go astray leaving God out of their plans. The people have been under-minded with information that is not credible information. It is time for the people to cross-over to eternal

God's Equal Living Conditions

life with eternal living on a paradise earth forming as the wrath of God's judgments and justice prevail with-out fail over the whole world. The old things of the world pass away as the new things of the world are forming daily to the good of the people in every part of the world.

God's Equal Living Conditions

God's Equal Living Conditions

God's Equal Living Conditions

www.ingramcontent.com/pod-product-compliance
Lightning Source LLC
Chambersburg PA
CBHW061757110426
42742CB00012BB/1896